NO FUTURE

YOUTH and SOCIETY

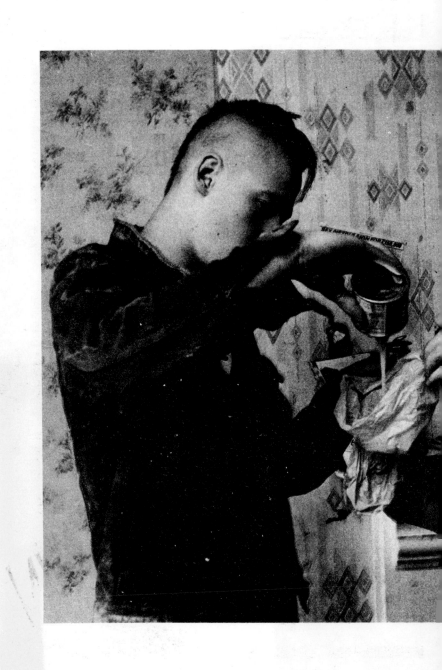

E. ELLIS CASHMORE

NO FUTURE
YOUTH AND SOCIETY

HEINEMANN · LONDON

Heinemann Educational Books Limited
22 Bedford Square, London WC1B 3HH
LONDON EDINBURGH MELBOURNE AUCKLAND
HONG KONG SINGAPORE KUALA LUMPUR NEW DELHI
IBADAN NAIROBI JOHANNESBERG
EXETER (NH) KINGSTON PORT OF SPAIN

ISBN 0 435 82164 4
ISBN 0 435 82163 6 Pbk

Typesetting by The Castlefield Press of Northampton
and printed in Great Britain by Biddles Limited, Guildford, Surrey

CONTENTS

ACKNOWLEDGEMENTS

The author and the publishers would like to thank the following for permission to use their photographs in this book (numbers in brackets refer to the pages on which the photographs appear): Simon Archer/Camera Press (ii-iii); Sarah Bishop/Photo Co-op (v); Fred Cicharski (3, 21, 89); Robin Coulthard (42); Homer Sykes/Camera Press (63).

One of the human prices paid for the current economic condition is the widespread loss of confidence in the future felt by workingclass youth. Violence, indifference between people, drug dependency, mental illness, even suicide; these are all symptoms of the changes experienced by youth. Workingclass kids today are being drained of their function and purpose.

This book is an attempt to make some sense of the experiences of those kids. I've tried to do this by first looking at history of youth in the UK since the Second World War and noting how social changes affected youth. To get information on the contemporary scene, I simply went out and talked to young people; I detailed their thoughts and linked them to their social circumstances. It took me six months of drifting around the West Midlands, particularly its dole offices. During those six months, I was a member of the SSRC Research Unit on Ethnic Relations at Saltley and I'd like to thank that unit for allowing me the freedom to pursue my own research objectives (though this book in no way represents the collective view of the unit).

I owe a debt to all those kids whose patience I tried whilst doing the research. Special thanks go to Mark, an unemployed youth from Small Heath, Birmingham, whose story links the book's chapters. Many readers will find Mark's story disagreeable. However unpleasant, it is real. And it's not the only unpleasant aspect of this book; it's not meant to make cosy reading; it's meant to convey the harshness of life as it is at street level. In order to do this, I've let the kids speak for themselves, giving their own views, expressing their own thoughts. At the same time, I offer explanations of why *I* consider they think and act the way they do.

In a way, this book is an extension of my previous work on rastas, black youth and, more generally, race relations. This time, I've tried to broaden the scope to make a statement on all modern youth, though the reader will notice I pay particular attention to the race issue as it surfaces amongst modern youth.

Many friends and colleagues read through and commented on an earlier draft of the book, so I want to thank (in alphabetical order) Carl Bagley, David Hill, Gita Jairaj, Dave Podmore and Barry Troyna.

EC

AUTHOR'S NOTE

With no future there cannot be sin.

Sex Pistols, *God Save the Queen**

Tell me what's so bad about trying to
feel so good,
I'd like a better life and I'd like to
buy one if I could . . .
Trying to fill the luxury gap has pushed
me to the brink.

Heaven 17, *Key to the World**

MARK
GETTING YOUR OWN BACK

Your name is Mark. It's 1974 and you're 11. You live in the Small Heath district of Birmingham along with your parents and five brothers – three older – and sister.

Tom is the eldest: he's 17 and works as an apprentice engineer for a firm in the city. Gary is 16 and he's just got fixed up with a job making window frames. All the others are still at school, two at the same school as you; they don't like it any more than you do.

The old man's a fitter at a factory in Birmingham. You don't see that much of him, as he's gone to work by the time you get up. And he's always home late. And even then, he doesn't speak much; just tells you and the others to shut up when he's watching the TV or occasionally bawls out your mum for something or other. He sometimes works on a Saturday morning. When he comes home in the afternoon, his breath smells and he eats, then goes to sleep on the settee. There's hell to pay if you wake him, so you make yourself scarce: go to a football match – Birmingham City.

Some of the kids go all over the country watching 'the Blues' play, but you've no money, so that's no good. But it's good at the match. The old man used to take you and one or two of your brothers, but he doesn't bother nowadays – he just sleeps all the time.

There's a kid at school and he reckons his dad takes him to the game every week, sitting in the main stand, as well. And he goes in a car to the away matches sometimes. Fat chance of that happening to you. You've got as much chance as playing in the Birmingham first team. Still, you can dream.

Like your old man, your mum works, but only afternoons: she does some cleaning at a works canteen or something like that. Some of the kids' mothers collect them from school, but yours doesn't; you wait for your elder brother, Anthony, and he walks home with you. It takes only twenty minutes.

Everybody seems to ask you, 'How are you getting on at school?' or, 'How do you like school?' The usual answer is, 'It's all right, I suppose.' But, it isn't; it's a joke. No one's really interested in any of the subjects – except games, that is. It's good on Wednesday afternoons when you get to play football. But otherwise, it's just something you have to get up early for. Only a couple of the teachers are okay. The rest are rotten. They don't teach you anything; they don't care, either. So why should you care? Some of the older kids bunk off school. They wag it: have the odd day off and go to the park or just doss around town. It's better than sitting behind your desk. You hate school.

One night, you and a couple of mates are hanging about with nothing to do. The old man is at home watching the television and the old girl is playing bingo at this club she goes to. You're bored. 'Let's go down the school and have mess-about', says Darren James — he's one of your mates. The three of you go just for the crack.

James is always getting into trouble at school: he's a good lad. It's dark, so no one sees him climb over the school gates. 'Come on you pair!', he whispers, but in a sort of loud voice. You and your other pal follow him. Quick as a flash, James has shot round the back of the school and has shinned up a drainpipe. 'What are you doing, James?', you ask him. 'Watch me!'

Next thing, he's yanking at a window, but it won't budge. He asks you to hand him a piece of metal. 'Quick!' You sort round and find an old piece of tube; it looks like it was part of a bike once. It's barely in James's hands before he's smashed it through a window. It's so quick it's unbelievable, but James has forced his hand in, opened the window and climbed through it. You look at your other mate, shrug your shoulders and follow him. Anything for a bit of fun; just for the crack.

Maybe it's the excitement of the situation, but once you're in the school, all you want to do is damage it. Into the nearest classroom. Over go the desks, posters are ripped off the wall, books are knocked off the shelves. You gob on the blackboard, piss on the floor. It's like a frenzy and you're all laughing as you charge into the gym area. Out comes all the equipment. Anything you can damage gets damaged. Then into the toilets; plugs go in the sinks and all the taps are turned on. James is trying to smash the mirrors with his pen knife. 'Wreck it, wreck it', he shouts. He wants to set fire to the place, but no one's got any matches, so flooding will have to do. It's a way of getting your own back.

Next morning, when you get to school, all the kids are waiting in the playground. You know why, but of course you're not letting on. After about an hour, you're all sent home. If it achieved nothing else, it got everybody a day off school, so they should be thankful. Only a day, mind you, 'cause you were all back to normal the day after.

The police came round and questioned everybody, and they even went to some kids' houses. Not yours. No one said anything. They still don't know who did it . . ..

1

LIVING IN A VOID

INTRODUCTION

If you grew up in the inner city with parents you never really knew and didn't have much respect for, endured the boredom of school, the soul-destruction of detention centres and the depression of unemployment, you'll know what kind of kid Mark is. If you were well treated by your folks, went to a private school or were tucked away in the middleclass safety of the suburbs, let me provide more notes, appropriately in police charge-sheet form. One of the smallest kids in school and the neighbourhood and, also, one of the most feared . . . rarely found alone . . . roved the streetcorners and made a habit of pouncing on kids who looked to have weak knees, then graduated to anyone resembling an Asian, 'pakis' to him . . . ripped off car aerials at first . . . then graduated to cars themselves . . . ran with his mates, mostly after pakis or away from the old bill . . . made daily visits to the headmaster's office until patience gave way to common sense and he just got ignored . . . so he ignored his school and stayed away . . . joy rides in 'borrowed' cars became one of the central types of entertainment . . . received no discipline at home . . . parents eventually became a distant memory . . . sometimes ended up drunk, sometimes drugged on amphetamines, sometimes got arrested . . . sometimes got locked up.

The details of the rest of his story preface each of the subsequent chapters. There isn't a conclusion, but, if there were, it would probably be that Mark became a hardened recidivist; his life will become punctuated with ever-lengthening stays in prison. I don't dwell on Mark's experience because he's typical of workingclass youth of the inner city; maybe he's not. On the other hand, he isn't one in a million either. He's a living caricature – a grotesque exaggeration of the characteristics shared by many youths in a modern society. He started fighting at about 11, stealing seriously at 12 and getting detained at Her Majesty's pleasure at 14. He was a father at 16. 'I got myself into so much shit by the time I was 16, I thought nothing could be worse than this. If I get thrown back inside, it's not going to be so bad. I'll survive. There's nothing else to do anyway.'

Consider the following facts:

(1) In the UK today there are 8.2 million people aged 13–21.
(2) They represent almost 15 per cent of the total population.
(3) Two-thirds are workingclass, males outnumbering females by 200,000.
(4) Nearly two million of them are on the dole.
(5) 12 per cent of school-leavers have no qualifications.

The young people of the 1980s face a unique configuration of problems which makes their position in society unprecedented. They're growing up in a society in which all the main institutions – including the schools they leave and the occupations they are supposed to, but can't, enter – have suffered a loss of legitimacy and are increasingly incapable of commanding the allegiance of the youth. Education can't fulfil its promises of good qualifications and work with decent pay, conditions and job satisfaction. So the motivation to excel at school is diminishing and the quest for work is becoming little more than a tiresome, meaningless ritual. Probably the most important aspect of this is that the young people of today recognize this as sharply – no, more sharply – than anyone else.

In 1982 a hit record by the band Musical Youth began: 'This generation rules the nation.' Wrong. The generation of the 1980s rules nothing – not even its own destiny. Like Mark, modern youths are being swept along on a tide of hopelessness. They have few ambitions, limited horizons, minimal prospects and no future. This book is about them. It's about the strangulating sense of futility which is permeating the inner cities, a sense of futility which makes modern youths cease in their quest for careers, let alone self-fulfilment.

Hopelessness is written across the faces of those youths populating the dole queues. 'You can't fool the youth', says the song; and it's right: these people know that they are living in a void. They are in a structureless situation which threatens to leave them useless, idle and dissipated – a void generation. And they know it. Take Tommy, who hadn't worked for two years after leaving school: 'I used to hear all the bollocks from the careers master and the teachers, "get youself a trade, some training behind you" and all that. And, honestly, I did want to learn something. I didn't just wanna doss about and do nothing. You might as well stay at school if you wanna do that.'

Yet countless unsuccessful interviews over the first six months after leaving school, plus a somewhat meaningless period on a Youth Opportunies Programme (YOP) gave him paralysis of ambition: 'I don't even bother looking for work now; they (the Department of Employment) never have anything to send you to. So what do you do? Nothing, basically. Waste.'

The youth of the 1980s are having their ambitions paralysed to the extent that they are rapidly losing interest in society, its institutions and the parts they might have been expected to play in those institutions ten years ago. This generation is different, very different from the ones that preceded it. Their experience and perceptions are different.

Young people in the period before the 1950s were geared to work, youth being centrally a transitory period, a passage to adulthood and the rewards and responsibilities it brings. Important features of life would be such things as the father's job, his earning capacity, your job and prospects, the status and respectability being a wage-earner bestow. Leisure experiences might even be linked to work. Work was the main life experience. The youth of the 1960s was one of the most vigorous manifestations of a self-conscious group-in-itself: young people deliberately elevated their age to emphasize their uniqueness; they dressed in a way designed to alert others to the fact that they were young and were different. These were the children of affluence. Jobs were in abundance and they would have depended heavily on them for the source of their money. Being a wage-earner was not important in itself but earning wages was; wages paid for the relatively expensive clothes, the scooters or motor cycles, the entrance to clubs. In both instances, work was vital, either as an orienting focus for life or as a vehicle for money. Youths' aspirations were pumped up to buy commercial products and work provided them with the necessary cash.⅄

For a youth of the 1980s, work assumes a different status: it's not a focus, more a dim image composed of hearsay accounts of others and job advertisements which never seem to have a job behind them. Work has become intangible. In extreme instances, youths even have trouble conceiving what it's about. Like Ronnie, who hadn't worked in five years since leaving school in 1978: 'I never even think about work, now. When I was at school and just after I left, I tried a few jobs, even went for some interviews. Then after a bit, I stopped thinking about it (a job). . . . Now, I just can't imagine what it's like to get up and go to work. I suppose it's like living in another country you've never been to.'

The modern account of experience and perceptions typically includes references to leisure, recreation, dossing (doing nothing in particular) and, sometimes, the futile pursuit of work. Sometimes.

It also includes the crucial recognition of an ever-contracting horizon of possibilities for the future, summed up by Anthony: 'This could go on for years – just dossing every day. Do I think it'll ever change? Why should I? I finished believing the bullshit. You believe 'em (careers officers *et al.*) at first, but not now. It's getting worse all the time. I don't feel lucky.'

That's after two-and-a-half years of job searching. The exercise absorbs the kinds of fresh energies driving some school-leavers. 'I'm not going to doss', claimed Jimmy just before he was about to leave school. 'I'm going to the Job Centre and I'm gonna keep going back and back till they find me a job.' Six months later he was still drawing dole, his spirit not broken, but under pressure. 'Not as I thought, but I'm still trying.' In another six months though?

There is a mood of fatalism spreading amongst the youth of the inner cities; it is a mood hewn out of the experience of persistent failure to find meaningful, gainful employment. It is a mood which is spreading amongst boys and girls, blacks and whites; and it is a destructive, debilitating force. This book is about fatalism and youth. It documents the crumbling plausibility of the view that maturity brings enrichment and stability and that life fans open into new possibilities as the years advance. Modern youth are forming the opposite view: that life as it's lived now is much as it will be in years to come – impoverished, precarious, narrow and restrictive.

In some areas of the UK, an average of ten school-leavers chase every one job opportunity. For the nine unsuccessful chasers, there will be the prospect of a long spell of inactivity which means no experience or training, which, in turn, devalues their credibility next time they go for a job. So they find themselves in a downward, ever-tightening spiral: every job missed means a tighter squeeze for the next job. The self-strangulating process is summed up by Bruce, a 20-year-old son of a postman: 'I went for my first interview three months after leaving school (he got four CSEs); it was to be a welder. I didn't get it. But I still fancied being a welder or something like that – I was good at metalwork at school, you know – and another job like it came up a few months later. But when I said I was on the dole and had been since I left school, they said they were looking for somebody with experience and that did it more or less. So, I've been for another couple of jobs since. Like the one at a bakery; and even they said, "Got any experience in this game?" And they gave it to a kid who'd worked nights a few months before on the ovens. I think he was bullshitting them, but that's what you've gotta do.'

In other cases, the realization that the lack of experience forced by unemployment will restrict the chances of getting a job prompts new postures. An obvious example would be changing career aspirations, like Nick from Kidderminster, who left school to train as a chef and trained for a year at college in Worcester. 'Then I got laid off and was out of work for months', he reflected. 'I virtually knew that all the training I'd done was no use after that 'cause there were no kitchen jobs going. So I just got a factory job – labouring and such like. I kept looking for work as a chef for about two months, then I thought "forget it".' In another six months, he was out of work again. A year later he was 19 and still out of work, but with a rationalized outlook: 'I don't particularly want work now. If it was a job like the last one, in a factory, getting bored, shoving metal boxes about or working machines, then I'd prefer this (the dole).'

Both Bruce and Nick saw quite clearly the consequences of their lack of working experience: limited chances of getting a job of any kind, virtually no chance of getting the kind of job they wanted when they left school, absolutely no chance of getting a job with a meaningful future connected to it. 'We're on the scrapheap already', said Bruce implicating his generation. 'We can't do nothing, we're not trained to do nothing and nobody wants useless fuckers, do they?' They don't.

Despite Bruce's statement, not all of his generation are 'on the scrap-heap', and it would be facile to write about youth solely in terms of unemployment. A great many are gainfully, if not meaningfully, employed and don't suffer the consequences of long spells without work. Yet the evidence suggests that more and more of the 16–21 age group are finding themselves jobless; projections indicate that this group will become a permanent lumpen group, fixed at the lower order of society with little opportunity to remove themselves from that position. That much we know. What I will add to this is an interpretation of how the youths themselves feel about their situation now and their futures. They are sharply conscious of their positions: some are hopeful of improvement; many are gloomy about their chances; most are fatalistic. The belief in self-determination and the benefits of initiative is dissipating; it's as if they think their lives are being governed by forces outside of their control. The accuracy of their assessment might be questioned but the impact of it on their postures towards society will still be massive.

We face the prospect of having large sections of the young feeling angry, resentful and discontented, thinking they lack autonomy, and behaving as if they have no interest in self-improvement. Born into concrete inner cities, the structure of which physically stifles their movement, they grow up amongst monstrous, graffiti-daubed tower blocks with broken lifts and dirty windows. They are educated in subjects they find irrelevant and whose meaning they find remote and quite separate from their everyday world. After school, they sink their early efforts into finding a job they're interested in, then a job that pays well, then a job that doesn't pay well, and then any job at all. The results of the experience are many and, in the course of this book, I hope to highlight some of them.

Having no work and sensing *no future* is the crucial feature of the present generation and, even those youths who are in work, can't fail to be affected in some measure by the changing situation. They will feel the pressure on them in a number of ways, such as in their depressed wages, the precariousness of their jobs, the poverty of their peers. They too will have their say in this book. There are the excessive fringes, such as punks, skinheads, heavy metal kids and affiliates of other youth sub-cultures and there are the mundane kids who feel little identity with any particular movement; blacks and whites, young men and young women. All will come into view. All share a common perception of a future in which they have little investment and over which they have no control. There are in these pages kids who go to Villa Park football stadium; those who wear tattoos and braces and those who wear plaits and chains. Some break the law only by riding bikes without lights, others regularly burgle houses. Quite a few are peaceful, while others are easily provoked into violence; still others are downright vicious and initiate fights on the merest pretext. Diverse as they are, they share one common feature: youth.

Here I'm suggesting something more than the fact that all the figures fall within a certain age bracket, say 15 to 21: I'm proposing that they have an awareness peculiar to young people in the 1980s, an awareness born out of a sense of shared plight and common destiny. They feel they belong to a category of people who are in some, possibly many, senses different from the rest of the population (even that older section hit by redundancies and lay-offs); it shows in their dress, their attitudes, their feelings, not to mention their economic position in the broad division of labour. They understand themselves to be part of youth and although we can accept such a statement in a matter-of-fact way, the very obviousness of it conceals the processes contributing to its creation. This book is about the development of youth and over the next several chapters I want to trace this by focusing on the peculiarly tangible forms of this phenomenon. The effect that youth subcultures have on their members may be central or marginal, lasting or ephemeral; but that effect is always there in some measure, and it is meaningless to write about youth without examining very closely the vivid forms in which young people have expressed that youth. Contrary to conventional belief, punks and skinheads were not at the outer edges of society, outcasts from the mainstream of the country's young people. Rather they were extreme even exaggerated representatives of larger sections of the young population.

In the next five chapters, I will survey the patterns of youth in the UK since the Second World War, reaching the 1980s by the end of chapter 3. All the time, I will stress the biting social significance of subcultures; they provide a kind of litmus test for the nation's young population. The analysis begins in the immediate post-war period when I argue there was no such thing as youth. Youth was created after 1955; after that it was recreated over and over again. The cycle of teds, mods, rockers, skinheads, hippies, etc. is a regenerative one and tells us much about the vitality and resolve of young people to stake out a difference between themselves and the rest of society. Doing the staking-out is a creative process and one which I now want to outline in abstract.

THE CREATION OF YOUTH

Creation? Yes, creation: there is nothing natural or inevitable about a segment of the population falling within a certain age bracket being what we call 'youth'. 'Being young, adolescence . . . young people collectively', is how the Oxford Dictionary, 1976 edition, defines youth, but this is a very abstract, vague and empty description based solely on age as a criterion. Most certainly age does enter into it, but there are other factors, social, historical, even psychological, which mark modern youth off as something rather unique.

To think of youth as just a phase is to swallow what the psychologist, John Dworetzky, calls 'the myth of linear development' (1982, p. 326). It's easy to assume that human development progresses in a fairly straight line at a steady, continuous pace: that we all pass through phases as we grow up, and we all undergo specifiable physical and intellectual changes.

But human development isn't nearly so simple. Of course, we all change organically, mechanically, cognitively, linguistically, emotionally and sexually, but even if some of these elements develop at a predictable pace (like language or body size), others might change in parallel and others may change independently of each other as the years pass. Human development is very, very complex and is critically influenced by all sorts of factors ranging from physical environment through diet to family background. The only aspect of human development that is experienced by everyone, because it proceeds at a steady, fixed rate, is birthdays.

So it's rather arbitrary and meaningless to identify youth in terms of age. Even though it's a fair predictor of human development, it's by no means a reliable guideline to all other aspects of the physical, intellectual and emotional processes.

Which isn't to say that we absolutely cannot define youth by referring to age. Indeed, in popular use, we always describe youth by age, say 14 to 25-year-olds. Yet this isn't satisfactory; a great many societies, past and present, simply wouldn't recognize anything distinct about that category of people in that specific age group. You're either a child or an adult, some societies would say. And to demarcate between the two there are rituals or ceremonies, rites of passage: on reaching a specific age – maybe 14 or 15 – the child is made to undergo a series of tests or perform a sequence of tasks in order to ensure he is ready for manhood (or womanhood). After the rituals, the child is a child no longer, but a fully-fledged adult.

'Every society must somehow solve the problem of transforming children into adults, for its very survival depends on that solution', write Leonard Broom and his colleagues (1981, p. 216). The rites of passage is one version of the solution. In the western world, more familiar vehicles for assisting the child into adulthood are schools, colleges and universities (the family is crucial, of course, in earlier stages). Yet only a small minority carry on from school into tertiary education; the majority are jettisoned into a world in which they are meant to pursue work. The school-leaving ceremony is perhaps the closest equivalent to the formal initiation procedures of other societies because it marks the students' acquisition of a new status in life; they shed their old status as school children and become adults.

Now this concept of adolescence is by no means universally recognized. Some societies identify a period of transition between childhood and manhood or womanhood, while other societies identify only two categories: child and adult. Schools are, in modern society, the primary preparatory vehicles for adulthood, and so function to produce humans suitably ready to join the workforce. The typical young person has a period of about two years from the age of 14 preparing for his or her occupational future, a preparation which is punctuated by marginal part-time or vacation jobs. It terminates technically at school-leaving, though for an increasing number its effective termination happens sometime before with the advent of prolonged periods of truancy.

Getting out of school is something which millions of students crave; yet actually leaving the school system brings along a whole new set of demands and, therefore, problems. The demands are contradictory and the problems are ones of adjustment. Let me expand: the child finishes school and is immediately planted on an unfamiliar terrain lacking the recognizable landmarks and features associated with school life. Life loses its old structure; systems of authority change; reference groups are different. Generally, people demand that you think and behave as a responsible adult. Yet no one has taught you exactly how; you just sort of fathom it out as you go along. You learn to be adult by a process of trial and error. Yet, on the other hand, you're never fully treated as an adult. You haven't the total set of responsibilities that goes hand in hand with a husband or wife (or, at least, a regular partner) and children and a home. So you're not *quite* an adult. But, just the same, you're thought to be moving in that direction, so people expect you to behave and think as if you are one while you're actually in the process of becoming one.

Often the demands are contradictory. 'You're old enough to know better' actually means you're now learning that what you've been doing is not associated with adulthood. The indictment might come after stealing a car and getting arrested (knowing better than to steal *or* get arrested?) or it might come after cheeking your father. Either way it means that you should perform differently in the future.

And these demands lead to a sequence of adjustments, all of which are problematic. Status changes are forced upon the newly-fledged school-leaver, and he or she has to adjust. There's no turning back; they can't say 'I don't like this adult business, it's harder than I thought; I want to go back to being a school kid again.' Returning to full-time education through college or university is a good alternative strategy, of course, but it's no substitute for the supported, structured existence of school life.

This is the state of adolescence and it refers specifically to the period in which the young person is striving to establish a free, independent, autonomous sense of self while still enmeshed in the web of his or her family. In modern society, economic dependency has been extended so that the person may depend almost totally on the parents virtually through the teens and sometimes beyond. The outside pressures, most notably from the mass media, are to create your own life-style and be an individual. One of the main characteristics of adolescence is the attempt to resolve this contradiction.

The American research of Kenneth Kenniston is interesting in this context: in the late 1960s he interviewed a group of young radicals about, amongst other things, their feelings towards their fathers and found that many tended to reproach them for their inability to act on their beliefs and commitments (1968). Kenniston argued that adolescence is all about a generational conflict in which the young people find the necessary resources to be able to break free from them. In another work, Kenniston theorized that youth followed on from adolescence: in this phase, the person loses interest in clashing with parents and tries to accommodate him- or herself with the social order; getting to grips with society not parents becomes the prime task (1975). Youth in this perspective is organized around the person's approach to society generally rather than specific individuals, such as fathers and mothers.

Adolescence and, later, youth occur in a kind of limbo phase. Originally, limbo was meant to be a place on the border of hell, inhabited by neglected pre-Christian folk and unbaptized children. The limbo of adolescence may not be as satanic, but the conditions of neglect, rootlessness, even oblivion, seem to fit, and the kids, at this stage, are certainly not baptized into the ways of adulthood.

It is in this limbo phase that *youth* is constructed: it is framed, built and fitted together as a coherent social category. I stress social because it's built not independently, but collectively. Young workingclass people experience similarly contradictory psychological and social demands, share common problems and, crucially, perceive that commonality. On the basis of that collective perception, they work out responses – again, not individual ones, but with each other. They combine forces to produce their own distinct attitudes, beliefs, commitments to society, their own styles, fashions, actions; their own clubs, institutions, establishments. In the process, they create what we call youth.

Now kids don't engage in this construction unassisted and, as I'll suggest later, they are very ably abetted by a whole section of capitalism which dedicates itself to developing an industry based on youth. Records, movies, discos, clothes, cosmetics, magazines – these are just some of the products geared to youth. A whole set of goods are packaged and sold to the market of the young; these goods aren't simply responses to a demand, but they stimulate that demand by manipulating the market. Fads and crazes in music and fashion are not spontaneous manifestations of youthful innovation; they are carefully nurtured products of the youth industry. Not that there can ever be a total manipulation of demand, as certain developments in the late 1970s demonstrate (I go into these in chapter 3). Nevertheless, it is fair to say that the whole cultural edifice we commonly recognize as youth is built by both young people experiencing broadly similar circumstances, and an industry only too ready to encourage them in their efforts to maintain that social category of youth. The youth industry, as we might call it, is geared to creating a constant demand for the commodities of youth, clothes, records, vehicles and so on. When kids are working and earning, they have the cash to be able to afford them; when they're not, they haven't. Unemployment in the 1980s created a disparity where many workingclass youths were encouraged (and are still being encouraged) to strive for things, but, at the same time, denied the equipment to get them by legitimate means. I look at the crucial effects in chapters 5 and 6.

What will become apparent when I examine specific forms of youth is that quite often the whole phenomenon is not based on age at all, but on other factors, inequality being an important one. Feeling exploited, discriminated against and subjected to unfair treatment and denied access to resources can spur people into organizing themselves and sharing a common purpose, and this may be unrelated to age. Now inequality may well overlap with age; for example certain groups of people in a specific age band may have similar experiences and feel themselves to be sharing a similar position in society. They may respond collectively. And how they respond defines their youth; yet that youth has no necessary relation to their age. Factors such as age, gender and class position tell us something about the conditions underlying youth, but not about the creative aspects.

Youth is a process of transition but definitely not a passive one in which the person is carried along on waves over which he or she has no control. The young are moved into areas quite alien to their experience because of institutional pressures, for example to get out of school and look for work. But, they also respond to those pressures, developing capabilities for managing their affairs and postures in relation to their situation.

Youth brings with it fresh perspectives on the world, new ways of perceiving and new methods of reacting; there is a continual expansion of horizons from the point of leaving school. Different tastes and motivations urge new experiences and achievements. And, of course, new pressures come to bear.

The combination of external pressures from the institutions of work and adulthood and the youth consumer market and the inner motivations propels the person and, in the process, stimulates the creation of youth. Independence and responsibility are thrust upon the young person. Yet at the same time, they are denied him or her. One of the principal sources of independence and responsibility is work: it signals breaking the bonds of dependency.

As the greater part of adult life is shaped by the concerns of employment, it's a rather serious matter when those concerns are removed. Entering the workforce is the critical early moment in youth. Not entering the workforce or, at least, having the entry delayed or continually disrupted, removes that critical moment and leaves young people in awkwardly ambivalent positions. Because increasing numbers of people are being lodged in this ambivalence, they can be expected to respond differently from their predecessors who were allowed to enter work quite soon after leaving school. Their collective responses are and will continue to define a new phase in youth.

But first let me offer some guidelines for understanding these patterns of youth. A start must be made by recognizing that people often share positions in society which they simply cannot change. Despite the American Dream that anyone with sufficient drive, initiative, talent and application can break from their social location and aspire to anything they desire to be, the vast majority remain anchored to their original positions, positions which are carved for them by inequalities in the distribution of wealth and power, in the division of industrial labour and in race relations. In many people's eyes, these features of life constitute a problem to which there are few solutions, save for a cultural one. What I mean by this is that most people do not directly challenge the social order, or 'system', through direct action, but respond to it by creating their own styles and formulae which make them feel as if they are protesting without actually making any impression.

In the tradition known as 'subcultural theory' workingclass youths' attempts to come to grips with their problems are gestural; they are symbolic protests doomed to failure after a short time because they never achieve anything tangible except for providing groups of young people with a vehicle for articulating their feelings. Workingclass kids, sensing their entrapment in an unequal system, hit out at that system. So, for instance, vandalizing property or thieving would be the kids' way of attacking the system; the acts constitute what David Downes called the 'delinquent solution' (1966).

Amongst the pioneers of this approach to youth were R. Cloward and Lloyd Ohlin who argued that, in the USA, children were constantly exposed through the media, schools and their parents to the view that they should attain success and status and be competitive achievers (1960). (The study was inspired by the theories of Robert Merton, whose contributions will be relevant to later chapters.) As members of the workingclass, many kids felt at a distinct disadvantage in the race to achieve valued commodities and prestige, particularly as they came from families that did not emphasize education. Educational success was seen as the route to social success. Daunted by the prospect of trying to succeed, the youths veered towards alternatives, creating three subcultural options: (i) the criminal subculture, gaining money through basically illegal means; (ii) the conflict subculture, gaining status and reputation by fighting in gangs; and (iii) the retreatist subculture, withdrawing entirely and indulging in sex, alcohol and drugs. These are seen as solutions, albeit ineffective ones.

In a different vein, Albert Cohen reasoned that not only did youths have their routes to success strewn with obstacles, but they did not possess middleclass characteristics such as individual responsibility, a sense of deferred gratification and a respect for property (1955). In response, they inverted such values and lived by their opposites, such as gang loyalty, hedonism, anti-property. Workingclass youth subcultures are inversions of what Cohen theorized to be middleclass standards.

These two American studies were important in focusing attention on the origins and nature of the youth subculture. Significantly, they both identified fundamental social inequality as a key factor, making sure that the fashions, styles and postures of the youths were in no way spontaneous whims, but part of a more general response to social conditions. Up to the 1970s, research into youth was carried out more or less within the boundaries set by these studies. Then there was a break, captured nicely by Stanley Cohen: 'the theories explained how and why kids would kick a machine; no one asked how the machine was rigged in the first place' (1980, p. 6).

Those asking about the machine itself as opposed to the kickers were influenced to varying degrees by the classical theories of Karl Marx – thus analysis began from the changing class composition of capitalism, and not with the frustrations or problems felt by youths. Culture, referred to as 'that level at which social groups develop distinct patterns of life, and give *expressive form* to their social and material life experience', reflects capitalist power relationships, 'so *cultures* are differently ranked, and stand in opposition to one another, in relations of domination and subordination' (Clarke *et al.*, 1976, pp. 10–11). In other words, society is composed of two basic, unequal classes, capital and labour, each with its own culture. Youth subcultures are seen as 'subsets' which have to be analysed in relation to the workingclass 'parent' cultures from which they derive.

The approach is exemplified by Philip Cohen's examination of workingclass youth in London's East End, where the workingclass community was based on an extended kinship network, and a high degree of social solidarity amongst the residents (1972). This depends on the geography of the neighbourhood and the work of the area. All these were destroyed in the post-war period when urban redevelopment, rehousing and immigration broke up the community. The problems caused by the break-up were experienced severely by the parent culture, and Cohen reasons that a series of internal contradictions or conflicts occurred within this culture torn between traditionalism and modernity. Youth subcultures emerged as an attempted solution to these problems. 'Magically', the youths tried to retrieve elements of the disintegrating parent culture by elevating features of those cultures. The solutions, like adopting skinhead uniforms and expelling outsiders such as blacks, are only imaginary, of course, and never confront the real causes of their concern.

Stuart Hall and others used similar theoretical approaches, insisting that young working people come into contact with the dominant culture (i.e. middleclass culture) in schools, in trying to get jobs, and through the media, though they themselves are born into a subordinate culture. They adapt to, mediate and transform the items of the dominant culture, effectively producing subcultural styles. So, for example, when we come to the mods, I will show that they were workingclass kids who appropriated elements of the middleclass in their style, trying to project the image of affluence and smartness in a very non-workingclass way. The long-hairs, or hippies, came from a middleclass culture, but prompted many of the focal concerns of workingclass delinquent subcultures, such as the short-term quest for excitement, the aversion to work and the rejecting of virtually all middleclass values.

The manner in which workingclass culture is sustained is pivotal. Paul Corrigan examined the relationship between school and workingclass kids: he argued that the school imposes itself on kids, controlling and moulding them to accept a view of society in which they can achieve virtually anything through hard work and application. But the kids themselves experience society very differently, as stifling and restrictive. So they reject the middleclass values associated with careerism and individual achievement and start resisting the school's regime. Instead, they 'muck about', playing truant or 'doing nothing' (1979). The irony of all this is that the 'counter-school culture' (such as missing lessons and rejecting discipline) fits in perfectly with the culture most kids are destined for when they leave school – 'the shopfloor culture' – and this was brought out in a study by Paul Willis (1977). In other words, resisting the school's imposition is seen as a sort of preparation for workingclass youth: they reject the things that school tells them, that they should work towards a career and try develop themselves as individuals. In doing so, they learn the sort of uniformity and sameness which they eventually experience as labour in capitalist industry.

Without confusing matters too much at this early stage, let me try to pull out what I take to be important strands, and piece together some theoretical framework in which we can place the development of youth.

First, and obviously, I have tried to dismantle any notions of youth as connected necessarily with age: youth is a socially creative process in which the young person, sandwiched between the restrictions of childhood and the often conflicting demands of adulthood, tries to come to grips with his or her problems. One of the central problems is that young people are perpetually exposed to images of commercial success towards which they're encouraged to strive. They're told that the rewards and prizes of society are distributed in relation to merit and hard work; so they're given approved ways of achieving those rewards (such as going to college, getting a career job, saving money, etc.). In an ideal world, there would be no inconsistency between the goals and the means for achieving them. Nice clothes, flash cars, good booze are things to be aimed at. But what happens when you're brought up to want such things, but then find you can't possibly make enough money to get them? The attempted solutions are not individual; they are collective and young people pool their resources, share their experiences, and work out common strategies. I will chronicle the various strategies in the chapters to come.

Youth subcultures are ways in which young people come to terms with the social order as they understand it, and frequently they articulate a dissatisfaction with the world as it stands. That dissatisfaction may take the form of a violent critique against the whole of society (à la punk), or it may be a forceful attempt to maintain a comfortable distance from the rest of society (for example, teds). But, whatever form it takes, the concept of youth is a focal concern: the people involved elevate their age to significance and seek to draw boundaries around their age group. This is because they perceive the problems as unique to them as young people and need to work out resolutions unassisted by those older or younger.

The resolutions are illusory in the sense that no change comes about and the members of the subcultures simply grow up, get disenchanted and resign themselves to 'ordinary' life. Yet, with a law-like consistency, youth subcultures continue to surface and resurface: the shapes and styles differ, but the basic thrust does not. Young working people persist in pushing their youth to the fore, and making it clear that they feel in some, often many, senses very different from the rest of society. Youth is their demarcation line. The subcultures derive from the workingclass parent cultures, and draw from the diffuse middleclass culture; there is never anything particularly new or original in youth subcultures. But the configuration, or the way they are transformed and put together again, often makes them compelling and vital, thus giving the appearance of newness.

Now it would be misleading to suggest that I can analyse all youth by taking account of subcultures; most youth, it could be argued, never get involved in any such apparently disreputable enterprises. Or do they?

Sometimes it's difficult to detail where the influence of something like the ted, punk or skinhead movements actually stops. Even if youths are not actually dyeing their hair orange, or sticking pins in their noses, it does not mean that they aren't 'into' the particular subculture. In a way, the subculture is an extreme statement of what youth is thinking, feeling and doing. Subcultures are often the vanguard, leading the way vividly and stridently, and articulating what many others want to say. Hall and Jefferson write of the majority of youth: 'their relation to the existing subcultures may be fleeting or permanent, marginal or central. The subcultures are important because there the response of youth takes a peculiarly tangible form.' (1976, p. 16).

Take something like punk: over a period of about three years, its ideas, styles and general postures were diffused across the whole population. True, this process was very much encouraged by commercial interests which transformed punk into big business. But the people who followed weren't mere automata, mindlessly following instructions to like certain kinds of music, dress in particular styles of clothes and develop specific postures in regard to the rest of society. Punk spoke both to them and for them; it refined and exaggerated the attitudes and postures of thousands upon thousands and its success was as much due to this as it was to the big business manipulation. So I argue, when reviewing the developments of British youth, that these young people were thinking out the problems of many and enacting solutions which were eventually copied by many others.

Youth subcultures are extreme, attenuated versions of youth culture generally; they emerge from the ranks of young workingclass people in the cities and give expression and coherence to the anxieties and concerns bedevilling all youth. Often dismissed as the eccentric rantings of a fringe of mentally unstable hooligans, subcultures tell us something profound about not only the changing nature of young people, but about the society in which they grow up and mature. Exactly what they tell us, we will now consider.

MARK
WHY BOTHER?

. . . it's 1979. At last. Now you can leave school legally. 'Legally' because you might just as well have left twelve months ago for all the time you spent there. You've been skiving off regularly since you were 14, but lately it's been more and more. In fact, you've barely been into school at all in the last six months. Your parents have had inspectors round, even the old bill has paid a visit. Still, who cares? School's a waste of time, so why bother going?

Most days, it's better in town. There's a bunch of guys who hang around the Bull Ring Shopping Centre. Most of them are unemployed, or bunking off – just like you. Quite a few of them are black; some are all right; others just don't talk to you. The old man talks about blacks all the time now; he reckons there are loads at his factory, but, as he's a skilled worker, they're not allowed to work in his shop. Probably because of the union. Sometimes, it's as if it's all he wants to talk about: complaints about blacks. 'Idle bastards', he calls them. 'They should kick 'em out of the country . . . send 'em back to where they come from.' He's been known to get up and move if a black guy sits next to him on the bus. The old man never used to talk to you much. He still doesn't but he talks more, not to anybody in particular, but just to anybody in the room. If you're there, you have to listen. 'They'll ruin this country,' he keeps insisting about blacks. But the black guys in town seem okay. Still, he might have something.

If there's one thing blacks are known to be good at, it's thieving. Everybody's at it in town, but they seem real clever at lifting stuff. You've been copped a couple of times for nicking clothes and records – nothing much. Some of the others make it pay, though: they knock the stuff off and sell it on the cheap. It's all profit to them and they don't often get copped. You're getting better at it, but, once your face is known, it gets harder 'cause people are looking out for you. And is it really going to pay in the long run?

Well, it didn't pay very handsomely for brother Gary. He's 21 now and doing two years for armed robbery. Actually, he'd been in and out of trouble since he left school: he'd done a few cars and a bit of burgling, but it was when he tried to hold up a jeweller's shop that things went wrong. You can see why he did it, mind: he'd been out of work for a few months and his wife was expecting a kid, their third. So? He took a chance.

You're beginning to take a few yourself, now, but nothing like hold-ups.

Just the odd bit of 'tea-leaving' and a blag here and there, like an empty house or something. Well, it's the only way of getting money. Not that you save much: as soon as you've got it, you've blown it. But, when you start work, you might be able to add it to your wages and put some money together. When? Well, soon now: only a month or two, then you'll be legally finished with school.

On the odd time you have shown your face at school, one of the teachers has given you what they call a 'talking to'. 'You're never going to get anywhere if you don't get your head down' and all that business. What do they know? The teachers and the headmaster – they all say the same thing. The careers master has virtually given up. You've seen him a couple of times and he says: 'What do you want to do? What are you interested in?' 'Birds and booze', you said to him once and he lost his temper and ordered you out. Who cares? He's full of shit, telling you to train to be an engineer, get an apprenticeship, go to night school. You know a few mates who got apprenticeships; they got laid off after two years. Anyway, who needs night school?

Getting a job shouldn't be as bad as they say. There are quite a few kids who left school last year who're still on the dole, but they're dossers; they don't want to work, really. Actually, they don't lead a bad life. You see them in town: they hang around the same places as you, they go to play pool sometimes, they might do a bit of thieving. They've got more money than you. So, even if you can't get a job, you'll still be better off than you are now.

But, anyway, you will get a job. What? It doesn't really make much differences as long as the money's all right. A mate of yours has just got himself a window-cleaning round, but they reckon it's all sewn up in that game. James, your next eldest brother has got a job in a garage. That might be worth a try.

The old man says you'd better get a job: 'we don't want no layabouts around this place'. But it's not quite as easy as that. The old lady lost her job the other month, but she got fixed up with another cleaning job.

The day comes when you can legally say you've left school. You size up the situation at the Job Centre. Now for a job . . .

MIMICKING ADULTS, 1945–54

Perhaps the most striking feature of youth in this period is its absence; youth as we understand it today simply did not exist. Of course there were broad bands of young people growing up together in the immediate post-war period. But there was no sense in which this aggregation of people constituted a

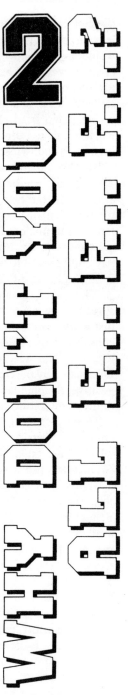

distinct social collectivity, a group with specific ideas and postures. After leaving school, the person, rather than slipping into a new cultural realm, would hastily follow his or her elders into adulthood without pausing to create a youthful existence. Richard Barnes writes of the very firm division of young people prior to the mid-1950s: 'They were classed as either children or adults' (1979, p. 7). 'The teen years were dealt with by a single step from childhood to adulthood', reckons Anne Campbell. 'Girls mimicked adult appearance by buying their first pair of stockings, high heels and twinset.' (1981, p. 117).

Boys would follow their fathers into work, frequently through the 'lads of dads' method (gaining access to a firm through the recommendation of the father); they would assume the appearance of their elders wearing their hairstyles, suits, shoes and so on in the manner of their fathers and uncles. There was no effort to stake out a difference: being young was no big deal, it simply meant biding time before receiving full pay and being able to marry and raise a family. In no sense was there a feeling of being different and wanting to express it.

Why? Well, the answer to this lies basically in the general agreement spread across the country in the period after the Second World War. The historian Arthur Marwick characterizes the period as one of 'social consensus', meaning that there was a phase of twelve years in which the legacy of the war seemed to unite people in their aims and views. Devastated by the consequences of the war, both negative and (for some) positive, the population started to piece life back into a pattern and, in so doing, they conformed.

Those just reaching adolescence would have spent their formative childhood years in a war-riddled state and were growing up in a time when living standards were improving despite the fact that much of the country was still affected by an economic depression.

Many of the conditions of war were continuing so that materials and foodstuffs were still scarce, but, as with many other parts of the world, Britain was rebuilding and so making the best possible use of what was available. Economic salvation hinged on the expansion of export markets; hence domestic production had to be examined. It was a period marked by the austerity of war, tempered by the relief wrought out of the end of conflict, plus the enthusiasm accompanying the beginning of a new age. Jobs were in abundance and energies were ploughed into filling them (see *The Age of Affluence* by Bogdanor and Skidelsky, 1970).

The war effort spilled over into the after-war years with people 'pulling together' not to stave off the enemy this time, but to reconstruct a new, improved future. So the period was one of relative social harmony and the consensus of the majority provided the opportunity for post-war reforms to be worked out. As production was so vitally important to the

rebuilding effort, both major political parties r
avoiding the kinds of mass unemployment that c
and introduce diffidence and fecklessness amongs.
Unity was seen as the key to this rebuilding, and this wa.
low level of industrial disputes. Loyalty to the established or.
was very strong. For example, a study of the time found that 73 .
of men and women thought highly of the police, and opinion polls n.
early 1950s showed rising enthusiasm for the monarchy, particularly so
near the coronation of Queen Elizabeth II (see Marwick, 1982, pp.
109–10).

It was a time of growing prosperity when people worked eagerly for a
future rich with promise, but promise that could be realized only by
hard, unified work. And this came about because of the general feeling of
well-being amongst the workingclass.

Marwick senses a security, even complacency, amongst the workingclass (which we will define as that 60 per cent of the population engaged
in manual work of some sort, skilled or unskilled). He quotes a plumber
interviewed in 1951: 'There is so much work to be done and so little
unemployment so if the boss rattles at you or threatens you with the sack
you can just up and leave.' (1982, p. 47).

The point here is that there was a relative absence of visible class
conflict generally: differences were subsumed under the general productive effort and, in any case, the workingclass thought the availability of
jobs gave them a healthy bargaining edge.

Also missing was the factor characterizing all the later periods: general
tension. This was to arrive in the very late 1950s and carry on until the
present day. But in the dozen years after the war, the rebuilding efforts
were of paramount importance and tended to shut out other considerations. Young people had no distinct music, nor styles of dress or leisure
patterns with which they could symbolically oppose older people; they
were not different but simply younger versions of their parents. This is
precisely the type of inter-generational continuity which militated
against the emergence of the youth. Young people showed absolutely no
interest in being anything other than adults, a situation that contrasted
with all subsequent periods.

UNDERAGE–OUTRAGE, 1955–63

The significant feature of this period was the end of National Service in
1960. Under the terms of the National Service Act, an average of 160,000
able-bodied young men were annually recruited into the armed forces for
a minimum of two years. Immediately after leaving school, the prospect
of National Service loomed. The actual impact of this on youth is difficult

assess with any precision, but one broad effect would be to draw young people away from their locales, their peers and their family cultures and transpose them onto a setting where rigid uniformity, total discipline and obedience were the order of the day.

Some argue that the conformity-inducing effects of National Service were positive – and virtuous. How many times can you recall someone calling 'Bring back conscription' for soccer hooligans and other young offenders? In this view, an enforced spell in the army, navy or air force had a controlling effect on the person, instilling in him the values of regulated behaviour and the suppression of individuality. 'Teach 'em to respect discipline', is an obvious harkening back to the days of conscription. The view is a widely-held one and National Service as a control vehicle is still seen as a kind of panacea for all the apparent ills of modern youth. So quite logically, in this perspective, the finishing of compulsory National Service was the cause of, or at least a precipitating factor behind, the strange, mysterious and outrageous changes in young people from the late 1950s onwards.

Whether or not those two years of enforced uniformity and strict discipline at a critical period in physical and psychological development had a kind of suppressant effect on society's youth, we cannot be sure. But certainly, when they were gone, the response of young people was as if some sort of safety-valve had been burst. But Richard Barnes reckons that this was one of two significant events:

> For the kids, the two most important things were that compulsory call-up into the army for boys of 18 was abolished, and that hire purchase was introduced. This made it easy to buy a portable *Dansette* record player (gramophone to parents), to play the new smaller, more convenient records that had been introduced, which played at 45 rpm (1979, p. 7).

The purchase of a record player or at least the ability to purchase one, was a crucial symbolic development. Freed from the burden of National Service and buoyed up by a prospering job market in which they could pick and choose, young people began to explore their new independence and take new initiatives. The sense of freedom from restraint was enhanced by the availability of work.

'You can sack me if you want to', said Albert Conroy, one of the young characters in Stan Barstow's *A Kind of Loving* set in the 1950s. 'I'm taking me talents elsewhere. I shan't have to look long either; there's plenty of firms crying out for blokes' (1973, p. 118).

Young workingclass people stopped imitating their elders; they were exempted from the stifling two years in the armed forces and so had more time, particularly leisure time, on their hands. What's more, their earning power permitted them to cram that leisure time with consumable

items they felt to be distinctively theirs. Quite suddenly, it seem
mid-1950s, young people, upon leaving school, started to rej
formity and began searching in other directions for their life-sty..., and
music was inspirational to them.

Nowadays, of course, we tend almost automatically to associate young
people with particular styles of music: youth has not only acquired
specific tastes in music, but has formed a very close personal identity
with some forms. But it wasn't always so: prior to the mid-1950s, there
was no necessary relationship between youth identity and music and
certainly no specific styles of music connected with young people. Stars
of the 1950s, such as Eve Boswell, Eddie Calvert and Dickie Valentine,
had a sort of trans-generational quality, appealing as they did to all age
groups. Then things changed.

Enter the ted: rock 'n' roll as a musical form emerged from many
sources and crystallized in the USA before it filtered across the Atlantic
to become the focus of the young people called 'teddy boys'. These
symbolized in a most dramatic way the intention of young people to be
different and to lift this difference to paramount importance in their
lives.

Like most other youth movements, the teds had small beginnings:
Dave Rogers, in his book, *Rock 'n' Roll*, recounts how some street gangs
of South London had in 1953–4 begun to enthuse over the strong and
lively music of Merrill E. Moore who played 'the first music with some
guts to it to catch on in Britain': piano-boogie. The gang members
adorned themselves with clothes styles derived from men's fashion in the
reign of Edward VII – hence the name teddy boys.

'But although it was expensive, the workingclass youths of South
London began to wear it and adapt it – tightly fitting trousers
('drainpipes'), fancy waistcoats and a long, drape jacket which had
sleeves that reached over the fingertips, and velvet on the turned-back
cuffs and round the back of the collar', writes Rogers (1982, p. 3).

Bootlace ties, and crepe-soled shoes ('brothel creepers') were added
and the hairstyle, long, greased, thrown back into a DA (for 'duck's
arse'), completed the ted image. Boogie music metamorphosed into rock
and its players, such as Jerry Lee Lewis, Little Richard and, of course,
Elvis Presley, provided role-models for the neophyte teds to copy.

Enthusiasm for the music and the emerging ted phenomenon was
given impetus by the general release of two American films, both
featuring the incongruously aged-looking Bill Haley. *Blackboard Jungle*
preceded the more spectacular *Rock Around the Clock*, and the showing
of these movies were usually riotous affairs with young people
screaming, stamping and jiving in the aisles. Concerned by this
apparently incomprehensible disorder, many local councils banned the

films altogether, and other authorities detailed police to the relevant cinemas. In 1957, Haley toured the UK with his band, the Comets, and, predictably, the concerts were pure pandemonium. In a most vivid way, young people were displaying their desire to create a world of their own, impenetrable to adults and inaccessible to children. Here was a culture of youth, created zealously by young people yet maintained, as we will see, by other 'outside' interests.

After the 'early warnings' of the teds, the media got in on the act to make judgemental statements about the alleged crisis and create what Stanley Cohen calls a 'moral panic':

'A condition, episode, person or group of persons emerges to become defined as a threat to societal values and interests; its nature is presented in a stylized and stereotypical fashion by the mass media; the moral barricades are manned by editors, bishops, politicians and other right-thinking people.' (1980, p. 9).

In this case, the press started things moving by reporting, somewhat sensationalistically, the happenings at the cinemas and concerts and invited other 'experts' to climb up on the moral barracades. A certain Reverend A. Carter took up the invitation, announcing through the medium of the *Daily Sketch*: 'The effect of rock 'n' roll on young people is to turn them into devil worshippers; to stimulate self-expression through sex; to provoke carelessness, and destroy the sanctity of marriage.' (17 September 1956).

Teds were perceived by the rest of a startled society as 'folk devils'. Nowadays we can look back at old photographs and wonder: 'What was all the fuss about? They look reasonably normal young people – quite straight in fact, compared to the more bizarre figures of the 1980s.' But the original teds appeared at a time when youth was simply not recognized. As Rogers points out: 'You were expected to dress like your parents, enjoy the same entertainments, like the same music, even hold the same opinions.' (1982, p. 7).

The teds just refused to live up to these expectations and, in fact, went in totally the opposite direction, dressing their own way, enjoying their entertainments, their music and forming their own opinions. Altogether, they created what later writers were to call a youth subculture, meaning that the members or followers formed a distinct constellation of ideas, values and behaviours. The teds generated new views on the world, new standards by which to judge themselves and others; they evolved a unique life-style. For them, middle-aged people were different not simply because they were older, but because they represented a different level of society: older people thought differently, had different aims – they were 'respectable'. By contrast the teds consciously tried to be 'unrespectable': the American tag of juvenile delinquent was adopted by the teds and used as a term of some merit.

The rest of society thought of the teds as devils in that they were believed to be mindlessly violent, sexually depraved and pointlessly rebellious. And the teds delighted in these allegations. Indeed, they went out of their way to promote the image; it enhanced their detachment from the adult world and demonstrated a new initiative from young workingclass people who had not previously been recognized as a distinct group in themselves.

What then were the changing circumstances from which the teddy boys emerged? The lifting of conscription and the availability of well-paying jobs I have already mentioned are factors in the widening popularity of the teds. There was also an awareness of belonging to the workingclass and wanting to emphasize that fact. This isn't to suggest that the period in the mid-to-late 1950s brought increasing class conflict; indeed, if industrial strike statistics are anything to go by, class conflict increased only marginally (2.07 million days lost between 1955 and 1964). Still, there did seem to be a readiness on behalf of the youths to celebrate their workingclass origins on their own terms. They moved away from the middleclass cultural influences which were affecting their families whose new spending power enabled them to aspire to higher standards of living and surround themselves with the trappings of the emerging consumer society. The youths also profited by the high wage freedom, but used it in other areas: not to stabilize their lives with new houses, cars and washing machines, but to clothe themselves expensively and indulge in conspicuous leisure habits – without moving away from an obvious workingclass location.

That 'workingclassness' was expressed in a most volatile manner in the 'wog-bashing' episodes of the late 1950s and early 1960s. Immigration from the Caribbean had been increasing annually virtually from the end of the war (see Runnymede Trust, 1980, chapter 1). The presence of blacks in the major English towns was not at first threatening (though before the post-war wave, there were riots concerning blacks in Cardiff, Liverpool and South Shields in 1919). Then, as more and more came in, they began to be seen in a different light, not just as differently coloured people, but as outsiders who were presenting increasing competition in the housing and labour markets. In other words, the black man was seen as a potential rival for houses and jobs and, as such, his growing presence was seen as menacing.

This basically was the reasoning, faulty as it was, behind the Nottingham and Notting Hill riots of 1958 in which many teds were active. For a few years after the riots, teds made blacks targets for their assaults in much the same was as the skinheads of the 1970s and 1980s had made Asians theirs.

By 1964, the ted look in its pure form had disappeared from the streets of most cities. Gone were the drape and the brothel creepers; 'in' were the Italian bum-freezer suit and winkle picker pointed shoes. Yet youth had arrived, for fashions were designed and marketed and bought exclusively by young people and a whole music and entertainments industry had been created to cater solely for the teds and their follow-on. The media had quietened down their panic-generating cries and society had become accustomed to young people with their own styles, tastes and outlooks.

Interestingly, girls in this period had been less vigorous than their male counterparts in stating their presence. There were new fashions and styles for women, the most distinct being the lacquered cylindrical hairstyle called the beehive (later revived by Mari Wilson), but the subculture was predominantly organized around teddy boys. Working-class males were brought up to do well at school, gain some qualifications and get an apprenticeship, but girls were reared with different aims in mind; the basic idea was that they would become wives and, eventually, mothers. So the stress on their career and independence was not so great. Girls were locked in what later writers called 'the culture of the bedroom': they collected photographs and autographs of, and fantasized over, rock 'n' pop idols, structuring their ambitions around a romantic marriage and domestic bliss. (With only small modifications, this culture was also prevalent amongst middleclass girls.) Although the ted phenomenon was revolutionary in many respects, it effected no significant change in the status of women as auxiliaries of men. Perhaps the first youth subculture to do this came in the mid-1960s, though its beginnings were earlier.

SO GOOD, 1964–8

One of the popular musical forms at the start of the decade was trad jazz, an English version of Dixieland jazz. Those jazz enthusiasts who preferred the modern American work of the likes of Dave Brubeck and Charlie Mingus gravitated towards London's West End, where they held informal meetings at coffee bars and clubs. Gradually, they evolved a collective identity, calling themselves modernists and dressing in a particular Italian-inspired style. These were the forerunners of the mods.

'Easter, 1964, Clacton: a group of modernists scuffled with some motor cycle enthusiasts. The young people had their own boredom and irritation fanned by rumours of café owners and barmen refusing to serve some of them', reckons Cohen (1980, p. 28).

The fights probably relieved the boredom. Whatever the causes of the violence (and I will be discussing the general issue later), the newspapers, national and provincial, carried reports, some with melodramatic headlines such as: 'Day of terror by scooter groups' and 'Wild Ones Invade Seaside – 97 arrests' (Cohen, 1980, p. 30).

Feature articles followed and stories of two rival groups called mods and rockers spread. Just as the moral barricades were manned before when the teds emerged, so they were again for the mods and rockers.

Now it's important to stress that, before receiving what was to be massive attention from the media, the modernists were largely fashion-conscious young people who derived their inspiration from the original modern jazz devotees. As Barnes detects: 'Although a Mod look had emerged, there was still no sense of common identity that embraced the whole movement' (1979, p. 9).

The rockers were precisely that: people who still followed rock 'n' roll and modelled themselves on rock figures such as Gene Vincent and Eddie Cochran. After the press and television coverage, however, the nation's youth seemed to divide into two camps, each antagonistic towards each other.

'The creation of Mods and Rockers' is how Cohen subtitles his examination of the media's pivotal role in the development of the two subcultures. He documents how, over a period of about two years, the press, television and radio amplified, exaggerated and distorted virtually any episode of violence between young people and made them seem like battles in a monumental war: 'Hastings Blitzed by Mods and Rockers!'

Nevertheless, the mods and rockers of the 1960s were not purely artificial creations fabricated from the imaginations of media men: these were young people who were quite deliberately aligning themselves with one or other of the movements, acquiring the feel for clothes and the taste for music – for mods, neat, sharp clothes and black American music, for rockers, rugged leather and denim clothes and 1950s rock 'n' roll.

Society had to an extent assimilated the rockers; they were, after all, extensions of the teds, whose novelty had gone and who no longer presented a menace. The mods, on the other hand, were quite different. Here was a growing band of young people, self-consciously different, yet deliberately disguising their difference behind a facade of unastonishing ordinariness. As Dick Hebdige puts it: 'The mods invented a style which enabled them to negotiate smoothly between school, work and leisure, and which concealed as much as it stated.' (1979, p. 52).

Pete Townsend of the Who, one of the few white bands accepted by mods, illustrated this when interviewed for BBC's Radio 1:

This kid used to work in the bank at the top of the road who had very, very short hair, always had a nice suit, a very sort of clean-cut kid. He was also an outrageous mod . . . his hair was short, but it was also a very subtle French crew, it was also smart and in fashion. His suit was made out of Tonik which was very, very important – it had to be Tonik. It happened to be in that month's colour, which might be brown or blue. The lapels had to be the exact width; it might be a two-button jacket, or a single-button jacket; it might be a three-button jacket with the top and bottom buttons left undone – whatever happened to be the vogue at the time. It might have single pockets on either side which might be straight or slanted. There was a craze also for several secret inside pockets, so one tended to fold one's jacket over and put one's hands in one's pockets, holding the jacket open so that people could see that you had the right number of inside pockets. And yet he would still get a job in a bank and he obviously had to have a job to be able to spend all this money on clothes. And yet nobody knew but me and him and maybe a few of the other people. If you'd have seen him outside of a dance hall or a club, you would've said: 'OK, he's a mod'. But, on his own, you wouldn't have been quite able to identify him. It was a way people could be legitimate: fit into society, go to school, even have jobs and yet, at the same time, still be outrageously fashionable and in-crowd.

That 'in-crowd' quickly opened out and, over the two or three years from 1964, tens of thousands of young people affirmed their youth by dressing in the styles, listening to music and going to the haunts associated with mods. What began as a barely visible series of sartorial cues about taste turned into the basis of a new youth subculture. The feelings of thousands were summed up by the Who's *My Generation* which asked adults: 'Why don't you all f . . . f . . . f . . . fade away? Don't try to dig what we all say.'

Changing the exclusive modernist style into the very inclusive mod movement was prompted, in the first instance, by the media's amplification of the original Clacton incidents, but perhaps more importantly later by the availability of mod products. Specialist mod boutiques seemed to sprout everywhere, old style palaises (dance halls) suddenly became mod clubs, previously obscure American records by such people as Otis Redding and Dobie Gray gained general release. There was a ready industry waiting to capitalize on the new enthusiasm for all things mod.

Bank holidays were monumental occasions for mods: all-night discothèques (the name came into use in the 1960s) were regular occurrences and there were sojourns to holiday resorts, 'just to see if there was any action'. Invariably there was; particularly as the newspapers were, as Cohen puts it, 'sensitizing' people to expect trouble; unwittingly those same papers were issuing instructions to the mods about where to go for excitement.

All this happened in what became known as the age of affluence. The post-war prosperity had reached the stage when Tory Prime Minister Harold Macmillan was able to tell the nation: 'You've never had it so good. The workingclass was prospering from an average weekly wage of £20.30 (in 1966; it was £8.30 in 1951). Marwick calculates that the average weekly earnings (i.e. including overtime) rose by a massive 130 per cent between 1955 and 1969, and this is without inflation as we know it today. Earning power was enhanced by the relative cheapness of many consumer items, such as scooters, cars, television, hi-fi systems, etc. Britain in the 1960s became a high-spending consumer society and this was reflected in the habits of its youth. Young people were highly conspicuous consumers, dressing well, travelling in style and, generally, exuding the air of affluence.

The period was also one of liberation; it became known as 'the swinging sixties' because the new spending power was complemented by developments elsewhere. Like the convenience afforded by the availability of 'the pill', a revolutionary contraceptive method, and permissive society it was thought to encourage. There was also a general artistic and intellectual renewal in literature, theatre and film; social criticism and satire provided cutting edges for such vehicles as *Saturday Night and Sunday Morning*, the Alan Sillitoe novel of the 1950s made into a movie by Karel Reisz, which explored workingclass disaffection. The writers known as 'angry young men' (who were mostly in their thirties, actually), had earlier served to undermine the cosiness and complacency of the post-war boom by attacking virtually everything and anything connected with the establishment: religion, politics, culture and so on. It was a time of cultural change and this was both affecting and being affected by youth. Mods symbolized this, particularly in their adoption of pop art products, clothes, jewellery, furniture and anything else jokily made of new plastics in vivid colours.

Modism, if I can call it that, was both classless and asexual. Although most mods were from workingclass backgrounds, they tried to smother this with expensive clothes and habits; elegance and glamour were important. Maybe the majority had low-ranking workingclass jobs, but as Mike Brake points out, for mods: 'Leisure replaced work as a major activity, status was from non-work, and city night life took on a major meaning.' (1980, p. 76).

Theirs was an attempt to deny the significance of their class location and create a world in which that feature had no meaning. Like the teds, they had workingclass origins, but unlike them, they refused to recognize them. Also, whereas teds were totally macho, aggressive and protective about women, mods were not: indeed the word mod referred to males and females. 'Sexual boundaries were less distinct in the mod world, the girls with short hair, flat bodies and inexpressive faces, boys elaborately smart and unbutch.' (Brake, 1980, p. 76). It was nothing unusual to see a mod boy with eye shadow and lipstick.

The demise of the mods towards the end of the 1960s is an example of what George Melly calls 'revolt into style', meaning that the movement began with a fresh burst of youthful resistance to established codes and practices, yet ended up stagnant and ritualistic after a gross exploitation by the media and commercialization by the pop industry (1970). The growth of commercial pirate radio stations specializing in 'pop' music for young people signified the recognition of a new youth market. BBC Radio 1 usurped these stations, at the same time rubberstamping the arrival of youth as a legitimate and distinct audience.

Modism became a commodity and its original pretentions to exclusivity looked ridiculous as more and more kids bought scooters, had their hair coiffeured into French crops and got measured for Tonik suits. Even the word mod came to take on negative connotations: 'a little moddy', or 'phoney' were terms to describe the followers, or 'tickets', rather than trend-setters ('faces').

The seaside fighting stopped, the fashions were superseded by new designs and the scooters were replaced by cars (at the start of the decade 5.6 million people owned cars or vans; this increased to 11.8 million by 1970). As the exploitation and commercialization intensified, modism as a distinct social form lost its shape and the young mods, perhaps through maturity, became jaded. The press recast the devils as relatively benign characters.

Now during the peak mod years, 1964–7, there was, generally, good relations between white and black youths. Originally wrought out of an enthusiasm for black American and West Indian music, the mods' affiliations with blacks grew. Blacks were admired for their music, their dancing and their coolness; they provided a 'hidden inspirational stimulus for the whole mod style', as Hebdige puts it (1979, p. 54). The white–black stylistic liaison was to continue into the 1970s with another youth subculture, though this time with new dimensions more sinister than those of the mods.

PUTTING THE BOOT IN, 1969–75

The link between youth and certain forms of music was established by the teds and continued by the mods and rockers. The teds had identified with rock 'n' roll which was a predominantly white man's music, with some notable exceptions such as Little Richard and Chuck Berry; but the teds themselves were fiercely antagonistic towards blacks. Mods, as I've noted, enthused over black music and accepted blacks generally as cool people. In the 1970s, the skinheads stormed to prominence; they were heavily into the West Indian music called rock steady, later to be transformed into ska and, like mods, appreciated blacks' cultural contributions. The black counterparts to the skins were rude boys (originally a Jamaican sub-culture) and together they formed a vicious, reactionary alliance.

The first wave of skinheads (as we will see, they had a second coming in the eighties) had two fairly well-defined concerns: (i) the preservation of what they felt to be workingclass traditions; (ii) the repulsion of what they perceived to be deviant groups. On the first score, the skins attempted what John Clarke called 'the magical recovery of community': they sensed an erosion of workingclass community with its strictly demarcated territory and close kinship ties and wanted to restore it. On the second, the skins wanted to defend this so-called community against 'outsiders', those who were conspicuously non-traditional workingclass. Blacks would have fallen into this category, but they supplied music like *The return of Django* and *Long shot kick the bucket*, so they were exempted.

Asians, long-hairs and poofs weren't: skinheads made a point of attacking anyone who, in their eyes, was a member of any of these. 'Paki-bashing', as the regular beatings of Asians came to be called, involved 'the ritual and aggressive defence of the social and cultural homogeneity of the community against its most obviously scapegoated outsiders', according to Clarke (1975, p. 102). As the teds had singled out blacks for rough treatment, the skins did with Asians.

The long-hairs, or hippies, were also objects for skinhead abuse. They were involved in a youth culture of their own, one derived principally from the American 'flower power' movement of the late 1960s. Outraged by the US involvement in Vietnam, youths crystallized into a movement of passive resistance, retreating into a world of 'peace and love' (their slogan), turning on to sometimes obscure music and experimenting with consciousness-changing drugs. The movement took place in the 'freak-radical phase' of subcultural development, according to Ralph Larkin (whose 1979 work is a good guide to American youth subcultures). Vegetarianism and communal living came into vogue in the UK in the late 1960s, and the English radical-freaks grew their hair and dressed in such a way as to symbolize their detachment from society. It's worth dwelling on the hippies a little for these defined the first genuinely counter-cultural movement of the post-war period. What I mean by that is that the youths totally and completely rejected western society and its bourgeois–capitalist ideals based on economic greed, material accumulation and competitive self-interest. Hippies tried to rid themselves of hang-ups, as they would have called them, about property relations, money, sex and so on. They established communes where money wasn't valued and exchanges of goods were based on what you needed rather than what you could afford; sex came the same way.

Society was perceived essentially as something separate and remote. Its representatives were capitalist fascist pigs. But the hippies weren't interested in changing society: only themselves. So hallucinogenic drugs were a means to open new doors of perception; free love replaced conventional partnerships and communal living supplemented regular domestic arrangements. 'All you need is love', insisted hippies, who appeared in virtually every urban centre: 'love' became what Larkin calls 'a shorthand for elaborate and complex efforts to develop new forms, styles and intensities of being which could only come to fruition in a social order yet to be constructed' (1979, p. 54). That social order was never constructed and the hippies simply followed their own instruction, 'do your own thing'.

The movement, which drew it adherents mainly but not exclusively from the middleclass, countered the dominant culture, but never challenged it except at a symbolic level. It generated its own music (most of which was later adopted by heavy metal kids and called simply 'rock'), its own art in the form of psychedelic da-glo posters and head comix and its own eastern-derived fashions. All these were assimilated into an ugly and most unacceptable commercial package and stamped on celluloid in the form of the movie *Woodstock* which effectively ended the long-haired counter-culture and started the hippie industry.

Skinheads saw these groups as running in opposition to their ideals about community; they saw in hippies deviants who wanted to change rather than preserve the world, who wanted peace rather than to defend themselves. So, they integrated them into their repertoire of targets.

The other main targets were men who looked even remotely effeminate. Attacks on these were called 'poof-bashing'. Again, the feature is: change. Those who seemed to be homosexual were, to skinheads, agents of a kind of change in the country's morality. Asians were undermining white workingclass security, long-hairs were trying to collapse the tradition of vigorously defending the nation, and gays were introducing 'unnatural' elements which loosened the country's moral structure.

The outfits chosen by the skins revealed their general posture; 'caricature of the model worker' is how Philip Cohen describes their appearance (1972). They wore ultra-cropped hair, braces holding up either Levi jeans or sta-pressed trousers, button-down collar Ben Sherman shirts and what they called 'bovver boots' (because they were designed for 'bother'); in all the items were oddments from a traditional British workingclass look. It was as if the skins, in contrast to earlier youth subcultures, wanted to embrace a workingclass image.

But, almost ironically, skins integrated elements of a black West Indian culture into their style: the music, mannerisms, dance and argot (slang) were borrowed from young blacks. So, although the main thrust of the skinhead initiative was to repel undesirable outsiders who threatened the workingclass community, albeit a fictional one, they gladly absorbed blacks. Why? Well Hebdige's plausible answer is that, while skins were reacting against the post-war changes which brought affluence, rearranged the physical landscape (through urban renewal), but at the same time eroded traditional workingclass life, they saw in West Indians a culture 'armoured against contaminating influences' if only because black culture had been 'denied access to the "good life" by the colour of its skin' (1979, p. 57). Feeling alienated themselves, skins sought out a group which had been forcibly alienated in their vain attempt to build a bridge with an imaginary past.

But the skins' brand of workingclass conservatism was not entirely compatible with the accommodation of blacks and, in the very early 1970s, the alliance seemed to have become unglued as the revolt into style process turned again and the skinheads were thoroughly exploited both by the media, which depicted them as the new folk devils (not unreasonably in this case) and various other interests – skinhead movies, books and bands emerged and, quite soon there was a veritable skinhead industry both to cater for and create a demand. The actual people who comprised the skinheads probably abandoned their ideals and changed to less visible postures. But the phenomenon itself with the workingclass racist ethos lingered on and received fresh substance some years later, as we see in chapter 4.

... AND WE DON'T CARE, 1976–80

November 1976 was a crucial month in the evolution of post-war youth. Thames Television invited what they considered to be a sample of devotees of a nascent musical form to talk about themselves on the 'Today' news programme. Instead of a structured interview, the scene turned into a chaos of abuse with members of the band called the Sex Pistols stealing the show. Within days, punk rock became the source of a new moral panic. Newspapers quickly incorporated punk into their headlines and wrote of a menacing new cult which threatened to corrupt the nation's youth.

Capitalizing on their notoriety, the Sex Pistols and other bands loosely subscribing to punk used every opportunity to gain media exposure, incurring bans from record companies and concert venues for their alleged indecent behaviour – like spitting at their audiences or vomiting on stage. Because of the panic-generating media, punk was identified with vulgarity, violence, vileness, venereality and intellectual vacancy. And the kids loved it; to quote the Sex Pistols' line: 'We're vacant and we don't care!' (from *Pretty Vacant*, 1977).

The media coverage afforded punk enlarged appeal to those young people with little interest in conformity and no investment in society as it was. Unemployment amongst the young was increasing, making punk what Peter Marsh called 'dole queue rock' (1977). Youths wore torn clothing held together by safety pins, they designed asexual creations from plastic bin-liners and wrapped chains around their necks as if to symbolize their bondage; the punks, like the mods before them, wanted to be classless, but instead of transcending their class location by dressing up, they wanted to fall below class by dressing down, becoming lumpen.

They were rebelling against the way in which music and, therefore, youth had developed in the 1970s: glamorous and remote superstars commanded the adulation of the kids, who imitated them sheepishly. The punks rejected this separation by constructing a continuum between themselves and the bands they enthused over. Punk music and musicians didn't just represent youth; they were part of it. The reciprocal spitting at concerts signalled the link between the band and the audience.

But they were also rebelling against everything: families, work, education, religion, monarchy – every institution that seemed part of the status quo was rejected. 'Don't know what I want, but I know how to get it. I wanna destroy', sang the Sex Pistols in their punk classic, *Anarchy in the UK* (Virgin Music, 1977) and it summed up the frustrated, destructive mood of youth in the late 1970s.

In many ways a contrast to punks, but in other ways quite similar were the new teds, who came to light in 1977 when they staged attacks on the punks. It was the year of the Silver Jubilee and the punks were issuing notices of their opposition to the monarchy through such records as the Pistols' *God Save the Queen*, which was a best-seller despite being banned by the BBC. The teds seem to represent the good guys fighting back on behalf of the establishment. Their opposition to the punks was based on their alleged support for the social order as it stood and this was sharply at odds with the ritualistic urges of the punks who criticized everything, literally everything.

Although they resembled the 1950s' originals, the new teds were, of course, from a different generation and they were largely anachronistic imitators, enthusing over old records, collecting rock 'n' roll memorabilia and dressing in old-style clothing. Like the skins earlier in the decade, the teds avowed themselves workingclass British and thoroughly conservative in repelling the noxious, disruptive influences of punk.

Here we see the oppositional tendencies of post-war youth crystallized in two subcultures: punks as the destructive forces of new, wanting change for change's sake, but with no alternative vision; teds as the preservationist forces of old, seeking order and stability. Yet despite the repudiation of punks, the teds still shared with them a celebration of being young, being different, and loving an identity with a self-conscious movement with objectives, though ill-defined ones.

The teds transformed into rockabilly rebels and lost their cutting edge once the initial flourish of opposition to punks had gone. The reactionary force of youth, however, didn't disappear, as we will soon see. The punks lived on right up to the present day; their heyday might have passed, but, even in the 1980s, bondaged youths populate the dole queues of the big cities.

At the time of punks vs. teds skirmishes, a slumbering giant awoke. Heavy metal kids were devotees of the kind of electric guitar-based rock that grew out of the late 1960s/early 70s. The band Led Zeppelin exemplified this: they were enormously popular amongst long-hairs in the period and, like a number of other groups of the time, refused to change their style with musical trends. Their predominantly white workingclass followers admired their resolution in sticking to their original musical format; the band increased their volume and altered their chord patterns – slightly – but remained substantially the same: simple, loud and raucous. Other bands emulated them. From as far away as Australia heavy rock bands like AC/DC drew attention.

A claim made by heavy-metal kids, as they identified themselves, was that heavy rock never died. Well, maybe it didn't, but it only barely existed for a period in the mid-1970s, and it wasn't until late in the decade that it returned (from the brink of death) enlivened by a mass following of youth, their denim clothes covered in studs and appliqué, their hair long and wild so as to swing freely when they shook their heads in time with the music – what they called 'head-banging'. This head-banging was the source of the only genuine moment of panic about heavy metal when a youth died after inflicting on himself brain damage through continually jerking his head at a concert in the Midlands town of Wolverhampton.

But heavy metal generally failed to arouse the kind of hysteria or panic associated with most youth subcultures. This said, the heavy metal kids didn't actually do much of note: they went to concerts, very big outdoor concerts, and they gave the appearance of being threatening without actually being threatening. That's all. It would be unfair to call heavy metal conservative: inert would be more accurate. The kids listened to music which had hardly changed in fifteen years. Listen to Iron Maiden in the 1980s and you could be listening to any number of bands in the late 1960s. Heavy metals didn't want to change society; and, for that matter they didn't particularly want it to remain the same. They just wanted a little corner of it where they could introvert to their own sphere, escaping to a fantasy world in which they played imaginary guitars and shook their heads into states of concussion. They resisted nothing, challenged nothing; they were just taking what Ross Halfin and Pete Makowski called an 'escape route from the X-rated facts of life':

The almost tribal uniforms of denim, leather 'n' studs, accompanied by the wielding of cardboard guitars, provide a magic carpet ride that takes them away from the forever faded monochrome life that most of us lead. (1982, pp. 5–6).

HM was an enduring movement. Its rebirth (if I can call it that) in the 1970s presaged a long, sustained spell of popularity, unaffected by the media scaremongering besetting some of its contemporaries. The very fixed, unchanging nature of the movement contributed to its sustentation: it just went on and on, the music being recycled, the concerts reaffirming the same pattern. As Rick Parfitt of Status Quo (an appropriate name if ever there was one) said of his music on the Channel 4 programme 'Gastank': 'It's like a steam train, just rolling on while everything around us changes.'

Together, the three subcultures formed a triangle of forces with punks representing change for its own sake, teds preservation of the way things were and heavy metal kids total inertia. Punks, as I will show, underwent mutations and stayed on well into the 1980s, while heavy metal chugged on and on . . . and on. The teds were less stable and dwindled to a few rockabilly music enthusiasts; it seems they held their place in the gallery of folk devils only as counterpoints to the punks.

A kind of second generation of blacks and Asians had emerged in this period, almost challenging white youth to take a stand either for or against them. Skins were the most vivid example of a group opposing them, while, at the other extreme, others, punks, saw blacks as ready allies. In the next chapter, I will examine some of these very different, contrasting and sometimes ambivalent postures on racism and other issues.

MARK
THEIR OWN FAULT

. . . but it isn't easy as it seemed. Four months since you left school and no sign of a job at all. One interview for a job as a chef and one for a slab-layer. They both wanted someone with experience and the money was no good anyway. The old man's moaning already; says you're lazy as the blacks at his place. 'I'm trying my hardest', you tell him. 'There's not a lot about.' But he turns his back on you. If he was out of work, he'd know just how hard it is.

Dave is a guy you used to go to school with. His old man was a paki who came into some money and left home. That was when Dave was 8 and he's lived with his mother – she's a white woman from Birmingham – ever since. You and Dave left school together, signed on together and knock around together. Now you're out of work together.

The thing about Dave is that he hates pakis. Absolutely hates them. His old man came back when he was 12. He wanted to live with Dave's mother again. But, he'd been back to Pakistan, married another woman and brought her back. Dave's mum told him to piss off. There's nothing Dave likes better than a good scrap with the pakis. You don't like them much yourself and you're always getting in fights with them. Have been since you were about 13, actually. You think they're dirty, slimy bastards . . . scum. So what if you beat a few up? Dave loves it.

Not that pakis are the only ones you get into fights with. You're always in some kind of bother. There were plenty of punch-ups at school; they were a way of establishing yourself. Now that you're out of work, you've got no money, so there's nothing you can flash off – except when you nick it. Fighting's a way of telling people who you are and how good you are. On top of that it's good fun. Dave loves a fight.

Dave will be walking along the road and see two paki-looking geezers walking towards him and go out of his way to bump into one of them. Then he'll say: 'Are you pushing me, wog?' And you'll knock one of the others to back Dave up – you've got to haven't you, really? These pakis never seem to know what day it is. They'll stutter something and, before they know it, Dave will chin the guy and you'll have one of the others. And you'll do them all.

Even the old man has to laugh – and he doesn't do that much. He says 'you silly bastards', but he loves hearing about it. He reckons they have pakis at his work and they give them a hard time, 'cause they're dirty and smell all the time. They got one in the bogs and pulled his trousers off, held him down and rubbed Raljex on his balls.

Sometimes, your old man talks about pakis and blacks as if he's giving a sermon. He says that the day isn't far away when they'll own all the businesses and have the whites working for them. He reckons that we dragged them up from their way of life and educated them and now they're turning round and trying to rule us. They're starting by taking the good jobs. He's got a point, you think: look at all the restaurants and shops and warehouses with funny sounding names.

Whenever Dave goes to your place, he talks to the old man about the pakis. 'It's a pity people don't listen to Enoch', the old man says. But, when you weigh it up, it seems that plenty of people did. Well, nobody likes pakis, do they? There's always fights with them. It's their own fault: if they weren't here, they wouldn't get aggravation.

You're in a pub one night. Dave's there and so are another couple of guys. Anyway, you fancy a knock and there are some pakis sitting down having a drink. So Dave goes over to them and says: 'Get out of this boozer. This is a white man's place!' The pakis don't look as if they're understanding him, so Dave repeats what he said.

The pakis appear a bit worried and start talking to themselves real quick. 'Did you hear me?' shouts Dave, grabbing one of the pakis and dragging him across the table. The drinks go everywhere.

You get up and move over. One of the pakis goes to stand up and you push him down. Then, he gets up on his feet and you grab his jacket flaps. 'Crack' goes the nut on his nose and the claret spurts everywhere. Dave starts punching and kicking and the other lads come over to help. There are about six pakis in all and they're getting a right kicking. It's difficult to judge how long this goes on. Chairs are flying and glasses are smashed. Blood all over the place.

True, there's not much opposition from the pakis, but you might as well prolong the enjoyment while the rumble's in progress. But suddenly, the old bill are in. Two steam in and break up the fight and another two follow them. It's chaotic, and the fighting carries on, but this time it's your men against the police. Trouble is, you're getting battered by truncheons. What makes it worse is the fact that you're tired after beating up the pakis, so you've no resistance when the cops start marching. Down you go and all you can feel is a boot in your ribs again and again.

You're up in court the following morning. 'Threatening behaviour' is the charge. What a joke! The sentence is no joke mind: detention centre for three months. You wonder what this country's coming to. Three months just for beating up some pakis! Whose side are we supposed to be on? It makes you wonder . . . .

PUNK–TAFARI

Interestingly, during the 1970s, punks had struck up quite a liaison with blacks, as you might expect from what's been said before, because of their music. That music was, of course, reggae and punks seized upon it enthusiastically. Reggae in the later 1970s was heavily suffused with a rastafarian inspiration and was, in effect, a protest music. There grew an intriguing correspondence between punks and members of the developing rastafarian movement: punks wanted to change the system totally even though they lacked a firm vision of what they wanted to replace it with; rastas also wanted total change, what's more they had a name for the system – Babylon.

The rastafarian movement manifested in the UK in the mid-1970s, drawing adherents from young blacks in the inner cities. Originally, a Jamaican phenomenon, the movement grew rapidly during the 1970s in such places as the USA, Australia, New Zealand and Holland (see Cashmore, 1981). But it was in England that the movement established its most vigorous presence.

Basically, rastas drew their inspiration from the black leader, Marcus Garvey who, in the 1920s, preached the philosophy 'Africa for the Africans', imploring black people in the West Indies and USA to organize themselves for an exodus to their ancestral homeland. At some stage in his career, Garvey is reputed to have prophesied: 'Look to Africa when a black king shall be crowned, for the day of deliverance is near.' When, in 1930, Ras Tafari was crowned the Emperor of Ethiopia and renamed Haile Selassie, many made the fairly logical connection between the new Emperor and Garvey's black king, believing the coronation presaged the 'day of deliverance', and the mass return to Africa. Their conviction was based on the view that, contrary to Garvey's view, Haile Selassie was God and it was he – not

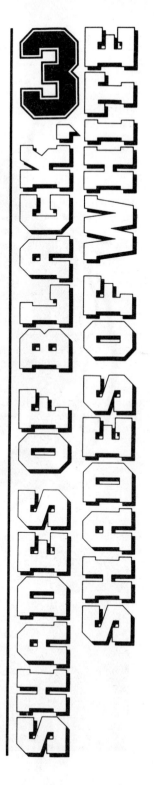

3 SHADES OF BLACK, SHADES OF WHITE

them – who would organize and execute the exodus, at the same time breaking the whites' world domination. In other words, the movement to Africa would coincide with the dissolution of the system called Babylon – to emphasize its inherently evil nature.

The movement's growth in England was unarguably the most socially important development in British post-war race relations; it became a vital source of identity and purpose for young blacks. Coiling their hair into dreadlocks and adorning themselves in the red, green and black of Ethiopia, they began to see themselves as a misplaced presence, sitting oddly astride the West Indies of their parents and England where they were domiciled when, in fact, they should really have been in Africa. This thought spurred them to new postures and they sought to detach themselves culturally from society, cultivating their own distinct way of life.

In many ways, the rastas fit into the same mould as many of the other youth subcultures: they were mostly quite young, drew inspiration from music, identified positively with each other, dressed similarly and, most importantly, emphasized their sheer difference. But there is another dimension to the rastafarian movement that is not found amongst similar subcultures: that is, it was a response to racism. Black youths felt themselves to be locked into a system which worked persistently against the interests of black people. Babylon had been formed in the early days of slavery and had remained intact, with minor modifications, ever since; blacks were not slaves in a physical sense, but they had to endure what rastas called 'mental slavery'. The movement's growth was inextricably linked to the perception of a world racked with racism: it wasn't so much white people who were the culprits, but the system of which they were part. The point was captured in the movie *Pressure* where the black youth, having grasped this point, remarks about whites: 'They're colonized too, just like we are. The only difference is we see the bars and the chains.'

Well, certainly punks saw the bars and chains and, over the last years of the 1970s, formed an affinity with rastas. The link, as I've pointed out, had its source in the music of reggae and punk–reggae clubs and discos appeared on the scene. But, there was a deeper level to the relationship: punks and rastas were both highly critical of and antagonistic towards the existing social order, Babylon. Rastas opposed it because its power structure maintained blacks in a position of subordination and whites in domination. Punks accepted the fundamental wrongness of this power arrangement, but thought they, as young people, were also oppressed, or to be more precise, restricted.

Punks believed the system was weighted against both the young and blacks. 'Rock against racism' concerts were regular in the late 1970s;

they signalled the willingness of punk and reggae musicians to use their music in the campaign against the rising forces of skinheads and organizations such as the National Front and the British Movement. No one ever determined what the punk doctrine was all about; it was a vague package of criticisms, very few constructive, aimed at everything. The enterprise had negative views on politics, the monarchy, morals, religion – it found virtually nothing to approve of in the social order. And in its place? Anarchy.

Hebdige calls punk a 'white ethnicity': 'It issued out of nameless housing estates, anonymous dole queues, slums-in-the-abstract. It was blank, expressionless, rootless. In this the punk subculture can be contrasted to the West Indian styles which had provided the basic models.' (1979, p. 65). The idea here is that punks sprang from the same well-daubed tower bocks and were educated on the same irrelevant curricula as young blacks and wanted to articulate the same kind of protest. But, armed with rastafarian ideas, black youth had a theory of history and a vision of the future; punks had neither. Hence their creation of important symbols out of mundane items such as safety pins, paper clips and chains. These were the elements of their 'modern world' and punks attached to them new significance: they represented a culturally barren world in which they were locked and condemned. Unlike rastas, they had no alternative of a culture based on a black Zion; so they took what was available and remixed the elements to create a new product. And that product was based totally on urban youth: punks decried anyone or anything connected with the established social order as Boring Old Farts (BOFs). They regurgitated the impulse behind the mod slogan of the 1960s, 'I hope I die before I get old' (from the Who's *My Generation*), refusing to acknowledge the validity of the views of anyone over 30. It was at once a celebration of youth and a recognition of the hopelessness of it; it pleaded for an end to racism whilst conceding the inevitability of its growth.

Rastas, for their part were equally as vitriolic in their condemnation of society, but guided by the vision, albeit a Utopian one, of a future in which black–white relations would be transformed. 'Must come', was the typical rastafarian endorsement of the imminent crash of Babylon.

The longevity of both movements attests to their lasting significance: a span of some seven years (at the time of writing) is momentous for youth subcultures, many of which are fragile and ephemeral affairs (usually the artificially manufactured kind like the new psychedelics who were totally products of consumer capitalism). Punk and rasta weren't short-lived episodes because they articulated genuine and deeply-held sentiments. They gave air to the bitterness, resentment, sometimes fury, of urban youth in the 1970s and 1980s. They, more than any other youth movement, reflected the transformation of youth from young people prospering in partially real but largely illusory affluence, proclaiming their collective identity and revelling in their lack of responsibilities and abundance of time and resources. The punk–rasta allegiance showed young people to be disapproving critics of society not youthful represent- ations of it. The continuing theme is that, like the subcultures preceding them, punks and rastas maintained their collective identities as youths and were, for the most part, impermeable to people who weren't young. But if the teds, mods and others were loud choruses of difference, but general approval with the way things were, punks and rastas were shrill, unmelodious screeches of defiance and bitterness. So what happened at the turn of the decade?

A general sense of a worsening economy, poorer living standards, deteriorating race relations and a collapse of the optimistic consensus of the 1950s and 1960s are obvious causes behind the changing posture of youth, though it would be unwise to try to specify a dividing point between the age of affluence and the period of decline. If decline is in any way measurable by using unemployment as an index, we can plot a gentle course from 1970 to 1974 with the percentage of the total number of employees out of work rising from 2.6 to 3.6 then back to 2.6; then, in 1975, it shot up to 4.1 per cent and, in 1976 it rose to 5.7 per cent. After a slight drop in 1978, it went up to 6.1 in 1979 and from then on into the 1980s and the days of double figure percentages. The groups usually most affected are: the young, ethnic minorities and women. From the first two were drawn punks and rastas. Marsh described punk rock as 'the music of the unemployed teenager' (1977, p. 114); it captured perfectly the emergent mood of frustration amongst the young. Reggae functioned similarly for black youths.

At one level, unemployment meant a reduced spending capacity for youths, black and white, particularly when coupled with price inflation. The days of affluence were over by about 1976; no more spending vast amounts on smart clothes and motor vehicles; torn T-shirts and Shanks's pony became the order of the day. But, at another level, unemployment was to have profounder effects – as I will explore in later chapters. Briefly, unemployment meant depriving young people of the activity through which they are supposed to derive satisfaction, their identity, feel some pride; it's that activity that's supposed to occupy the largest chunk of anyone's time between birth and death. Obviously, we hear time and time again of the boring monotonous, drill-like, alienating nature of much work; but, at least, as one youth put it, 'it's something to do; the alternative is do fuck all, all day'.

The conditions of job security and intensifying competition for positions were exactly the ones precipitating the conflicts between whites and blacks in the later 1950s. The contraction in the labour market after the immediate post-war expansion brought new faces to the dole queues. Blacks, prior to this time, were seen as auxiliaries in the sense that they were welcomed to the UK to fill in the gaps in the labour force: the economic 'boom' of the late 1940s and early 1950s had ensured virtual full employment and migration from, principally, the British West Indies, and, secondly, South Asia (India and Pakistan), supplied basic labour. The white workingclass prospered from the situation, enjoying freedom of mobility and a range of options; remember the 'there are plenty of jobs about . . .' example from chapter 2.

Imagine a department store with a promotion system based on its floors, so that, if you're the managing director, you work on the top floor and, if you're the tea-maker, you work in the basement. Around Christmastime, the store gets busy, so all the employees get a chance to move up. Those on the third floor move up to the fourth, those on the second to the third and so on, with the basement workers rising to the ground or the first floors. But there's no one to work the basement. The solution: bring in outside workers, who are prepared to put up with not-too-pleasant working conditions, without terrific wages and with long and often awkward hours. Everyone upstairs is happy, as are the new workers brought in and the store profits nicely from the system. After Christmas, however, sales drop and the store's management begin to cut jobs; but the basement workers have got used to their jobs and it would be impossible to fire them and funnel everyone downstairs. So jobs are chopped on all floors, some third-floor workers lose out, as do those on all other floors, including the basement. Now, those who've lost their jobs look at the basement workers who haven't lost theirs in a different light; they think, 'if they hadn't been brought in here in the first place, there'd still be jobs around, even if they were only those in the basement.' In effect, they don't blame the January–February recession for the job losses, but they blame the basement workers who've managed to hang on to their jobs. An equation seems plausible; it goes: if there are 100 jobs lost and 100 outsiders working in the basement, then those jobs would still be around if the outsiders weren't here. The logic of the argument may be flawed, but the equation gains credibility for the worker who feels he's pushed out of work by outsiders.

In the 1950s that equation applied to immigrants. If there's half-a-million blacks here, and half-a-million on the dole, then those blacks are the cause of the unemployment; if they weren't here, the jobs would still be open. This kind of logic propelled the teds and their accomplices in the 1950s, as it did the skinheads in the 1970s, but it's by no means confined to these and their sons and daughters. Scapegoating outsiders is a convenient way of blaming one group for all the ills of society, when in actual fact that group is in no way to blame and, in many circumstances, is more badly affected by the social ills.

The persistence of this specious reasoning will become much more evident when I recount the views of youth in the 1980s, but, for the moment, let me simply document the fundamental logic behind a lot of racist thinking: the outcome is to identify one or more visible and obviously different groups and attribute them with causes of deteriorating social conditions. Unemployment and general economic decline may be the primary causes behind losses in spending power, poorer housing, education cut-backs, worsening social services and so on, but it's much simpler to look for a tangible target to blame and hit. After all, you can't beat up social processes but you can pakis. And this is exactly what some groups thought and did in the later 1970s and early 1980s.

Unemployment is certainly not the explain-all concept it has been made out to be. Those mounting the moral barricades and making pronouncements about youth violence, delinquency and drug abuse amongst other things are quick to cite unemployment as the sole cause. It isn't: it may well be the single most important factor behind the excesses and problems of the young, but a full understanding can't be grasped without paying attention to the other elements involved; and this is what I intend to do.

This stated, we can certainly point to the lack of work from the late 1970s as a most powerful influence in the postures of youths, white and black. Punks and rastas believed themselves to be trapped in a plot of Kafkaesque proportions. Like a man caught in a bizarre bureaucratic maze with no apparent way out, many youths perceived every avenue of advancement blocked.

The critique of society as articulated in particular by young blacks was a very pertinent and trenchant one. At a general level, for example, a rasta told me how: 'I now understand how the Imperial Machine of the West and the religions that served it were designed to oppress all black peoples in the world.' More specifically, another rasta reckoned: 'I experience certain things: that a black youth cannot walk the streets without a chance of being picked up by the police, a chance of being beaten up by the National Front . . . we can't get a job because of our religion, the colour of our skin' (from Cashmore, 1983, pp. 130–1). In 1978, a punk told me: 'We're on the same side as the rastas. People think they're their own people, projecting their own image.' (Cashmore, 1983, p. 179).

The affinity felt between punks and rastas was based on a recognition of a common plight ('we're on the same side'), a resentment of the system which perpetuated that plight and a longing to change it, albeit through different means, though neither group did anything obviously constructive to further that change. The perception, however, was clear enough and the affiliation between black and white youth, though not strong, had been forged out of a common recognition. The link was captured in a piece of graffiti I noticed in a Birmingham subway: 'Punk–Tafari'.

It was not a lasting link, however, and it became progressively weaker as the end of the decade loomed. As with most other exploitable phenomena, punk became amenable to commercialization and the music and products were quite quickly integrated into what we might call mainstream pop culture: movies like *Jubilee* and the *Great Rock 'n' Roll Swindle* used punk themes; clothes shops all over the country specialized in punk fashion; punk or punk-derivative records shot into the popular music charts and the critical impulse was all but lost. The rastafarian package also underwent a kind of commercialization: parallel processes ensured that a distinct rasta commodity industry was built up on records, films, etc. Again the critical impulse was dampened but not entirely extinguished: a residual number of punks retained integrity of sorts and were assisted by new, unexploited bands and less commercial clubs and discos. In the 1980s, there was more or less a 'second generation' of punks: youths of around 16–17 (who would have been about 11 when the subculture first emerged) asserted the vitality of punk and its relevance at a time of severe depression for youth. Rastas continued to attract younger and younger affiliates, many subscribing to the general ideas such as the conspiracy of Babylon and the importance of Africa, without plumbing the theological depths of the movement in its religious aspect.

400 YEARS

The rastafarian movement continued to exert an important influence on vast portions of black youth in the 1980s. Even a small minority of inner-city whites locksed their hair and proclaimed allegiance to Ras Tafari as if to demonstrate their affinity with the black youths with whom they grew up in the inner cities. It became possible for a white band like the Ruts to release a rasta record like *Babylon's Burnin'*.

For the moment, let me determine that being a rasta involves the individual accepting two linked beliefs: (i) the divinity of Haile Selassie; (ii) that all black people should ultimately go back to Africa. Beyond these, there are no meaningful doctrinal points of unity. Some rastas won't eat pork; others will. Some smoke herb (ganja) ritually; others don't. Some insist that the whites' domination of blacks through imperialism is in a process of dissolution; others feel that the whites are as much in command as ever. The list is almost endless. In fact, one of the main reasons why the movement caught on in the UK was that there was no clear, unambiguous doctrine that the would-be member had to accept in order to call himself or herself a rasta. The rastafarian beliefs were open to interpretation – so long as the member believed in Haile Selassie and the return to Africa.

But, as the movement developed, many blacks dipped into the rasta beliefs and pulled out whatever they felt appropriate without wholeheartedly becoming a rasta. For example, a youth might fashion his hair into dreadlocks, but identify with the movement without actually being a rasta. One youth who did so justified his actions to me: 'It's I's way of showing my naturalness; of rejecting the western world's materialism and showing that I am a roots man. This is not rasta: it is natural to blackness . . . I can't accept Haile Selassie as my god. Christianity is my way, Haile Selassie was a mere king.'

The look of dread was immensely popular, but so too was the acceptance of one of the central rastafarian beliefs. In the 1980s, it was no longer necessary to be a rasta to believe in the existence of Babylon. This may, in the 1970s, have been an obscure way of comprehending the world, but, in the 1980s, Babylon was the reality experienced by black youths. Babylon was felt to exist everywhere: on the streets, in the churches, in the dole queues. Babylon became the single most important concept in the rastafarian repertoire. It provided thousands of black youth with a tool for analysing the nature of society and their position in that society. In a *New Community* article called 'After the rastas', I speculated on the increasing relevance of Babylon to young blacks and its role in promoting the kinds of awareness which resulted in the Brixton riots in 1981 (Cashmore, 1981). The basic problems of bad housing, lack of job opportunities, perceived harassment by the police were explicable in terms of the existence of Babylon: whites had kept blacks down and were doing everything possible to keep it that way. Racism was a main tool to this end: by separating out black people and subjecting them to unequal treatment in many spheres of society, like education, employment and the law, whites, it was thought, could maintain their grip – and so keep Babylon intact.

This was precisely the kind of awareness that spread amongst black youth; in the eyes of a young black person who found difficulty getting a job at all, let alone an apprenticeship or some sort of training scheme, everything fell into place in terms of the Babylonian conspiracy. What's more, the belief was contagious and even school-children, armed with ideas from the elder brothers and sisters, began to think in terms of Babylon. This was first brought home to me when I witnessed a scene in Handsworth: a group of two black youths and some younger children are walking along the street when a panda car draws up; two police officers spring from the car to apprehend the youths, corralling them into the car and driving off to the continual shouts of 'Babylon, Babylon!' from the children.

The disaffection of black youths wasn't at all caused by the growth of rastafarian beliefs. Rather, those beliefs gained purchase because social conditions permitted it: in particular, the concept of Babylon drew great credibility from the worsening situation blacks found themselves in at the start of the 1980s. They became aware that they had what Barry Troyna in his study of black school-children calls a 'shared destiny' (1982, p. 64). If they wanted some kind of comprehension or explanation of why they were in that position, they needed to look no further than rastafarian theory.

To understand the phenomenal rise not so much of the rastafarian movement, but of the general rastafarian ethos, the spirit and beliefs of the movement, we have to recognize two features. One is obviously the widespread availability of rasta ideas. Originally these came to England via Jamaica, mostly through reggae records – though there most certainly were groups of rastas in the UK since the 1950s, as I have noted in *Rastaman* (1983, pp. 50–3). Although in my study, few rastas would consciously acknowledge that reggae was the major inspiration, on occasion they would concede: 'I suppose music was my first contact with Ras Tafari; and it was this that made me look inside myself to find the true rastaman within I'; or 'I used to listen to music and sometimes a certain record might stick in my memory and I would meditate on that record. The words of it got stronger, began to make meaning for I' (1983, p. 106).

The first wave of rastas, say from 1976 to 1980, were stimulated to probe into reggae and use it as a kind of revelatory experience, taking themes and 'reasoning' them through in long, intense conversations with other rastas. The second wave of youths inspired by rasta had all the ideas available to them: the movement had, by the end of the decade, attracted a formidable following and had been reasonably well-attended to by the media – becoming the source of at least one moral panic in Handsworth (see Cashmore, 1983, chapter 10). But this doesn't tell us why more and more non-rasta black youths swallowed up rastafarian ideas. The basic answer is that they were rendered suggestible by the social conditions through which they grew up. This is the second feature we need to recognize. Disenchanted with educations they found irrelevant and unmotivated by families which failed to play adequate supporting roles in their general educations, black children tended to do badly at school and so finished up 'underachieving' (Taylor, 1981; Rampton, 1981; Tomlinson, 1982). Having no qualifications of note, they began from a disadvantage and so lacked the kinds of commitment needed to progress in a career. The situation was compounded by the outright racialism they encountered when trying to get on such things as apprenticeships and training programmes, and there is good evidence to suggest that this type of racialism operates fairly systematically (see Lee and Wrench, 1981). Then, the massive youth unemployment affected blacks more than any other single group. All the factors combined to depress the morale, drain away energies, generally, demotivate the black youth from taking an active part in society.

The rastafarian posture was one of detachment and, in the 1980s, more black youths are striking up this posture. Intrigued by the rasta analysis of society and its conclusion that it will simply not allow black people an active role, many blacks nowadays take the view that the basic rasta idea of Babylon is correct and that the system is working to the detriment of blacks. Faced with the future as they see it, who can blame them? The plausibility of rasta ideas is enhanced by every fresh round of school-leavers who will take their places in the dole queue, attempt to find a job for a few months, then sense the pointlessness of their search. As one youth told me: 'I'm not a rasta personally but I know many and they are all good roots brothers . . . I don't think it's necessary to believe totally their whole philosophy: one is an individual and one must worship as you believe. But much of rasta is truth, it is a philosophy of black people and I say it is a philosophy for all black brethren!'

The rasta explosion was like someone throwing a stone into the centre of a still pond: for long afterwards the ripples extended outwards towards the periphery. The movement's impact in the late 1970s was momentous and its influence continued, prompting many to favour the popular view that there were 'genuine rastas' and 'masqueraders'. To pose such a division is to mistake the nature and quality of the movement: there were never any hard and fast distinctions between rastas and non-rastas; no oaths, rituals or ceremonies to go through. Being rasta was always a process of becoming. 'The learning never stops', one rasta told me, referring to the way in which acquiring rasta knowledge involved comprehending the world in a different perspective and always seeking to add to the comprehension through study and reasoning. In my study of the movement, I identified the critical point in the whole process as the acceptance phase, when the youth accorded Haile Selassie with divine status. But perhaps my analysis was even then too linear: being drawn to the movement is not an inexorable drift towards acceptance; rather it can involve all manner of deviation. There is a kind of selective perception in which the youth sees in the movement exactly what he wants to see. So vague and amorphous is the rastafarian philosophy that virtually every individual can extract whatever meaning he or she likes from it. But the central meaning was captivity and repression. The whole rastafarian ethos was structured around these themes and they took on significance for the whole of black youth. '400 years' of slavery was how rastas described their condition: it was a description recognizable to thousands of other black youths, who in their own, perhaps idiosyncratic, way identified with rasta in the 1980s.

The effect growing up in a world of material abundance had on youth prior to the mid-1970s was for youths to form, quite self-consciously, cultures based on their age. Those almost grandiose cultures of affluence and expansion were supplanted by grimmer, more sullen movements based on poverty and constriction. Maturing black youths found their lives double-bound by the ropes of unemployment and racialism. The withdrawal of many into predominantly black cultures of resistance was both a response to this condition and a creative attempt to construct an alternative existence based on blackness. That many others were to follow their examples without perhaps the totality of commitment of rastas attests not so much to the inherent plausibility of rastafarian ideas, but to the willingness of black youths generally to seek out alternative beliefs and life-styles to the ones on offer. They had little or no investment in a world with no jobs in which blackness was to be disparaged and used as a basis for exclusion.

Very few black youths in the 1980s escaped the resonance of what the late rasta musician and, to many, prophet Bob Marley called 'rastaman vibration' (from *Positive Vibration*, 1976). Rasta was a main influence on the consciousness of young blacks in the period and continually asserted itself in the way they dressed, the way they spoke (in a patois), the way they walked even (a loose-limbed bouncy stride); but, most importantly, in the way they postured themselves in relation to the wider society. They grew weary of the futile search for acceptance as equals and so effected a sort of detachment, severing their links with society and opting out of the race for jobs, careers, security and the rest of the trappings young people are meant to aim for. Those goals and the values underpinning them were seen as unattainable and so blacks jettisoned them.

As one black youth, two years out of work since leaving school, said: 'You get told about careers and things when you leave school and then you go for a few jobs and maybe there's a white kid there and he gets the job and he's got no more qualifications than you; and so it starts you thinking . . . "Is it harder for a black man?" Then, when it keeps happening and your mates tell you the same thing, you know it's true . . . so you get to the realization that there's no point.'

'And the rasta influence?', I asked him (he was wearing the colours). He replied with a question which captured the mood of times: 'How can *you* deny what rasta is saying is untrue? Where is the truth in what the white man has been telling blacks for years? Where indeed?'

Before concluding this section, let me add that it's misleading to view all black youth as in some way involved in rasta. A less popular, though still relevant, subculture was that revolving around the music called Jazzfunk. This was a predominantly black form with the adherents eschewing any political influence: music, dancing and dressing were the important items. A great many blacks, uninterested in the rasta posture, opted for this pleasanter, altogether milder, subculture, creating for themselves a non-political world of sound and movement, music and light, where Babylon never intruded.

TWO-TONE

'The ghost town' is what some call Coventry, a Midlands city twenty miles south-east of Birmingham, once a symbol of post-war affluence with a thriving motor industry, now a degenerating indicator of the 1980s recession. It's so-called because of its desolation: the city centre precinct was the focus for so much violence that an 11 p.m. curfew was imposed, resulting in the centre's desertion after that time. Hence ghost town.

Coventry was overrun with clashes between youths in the late 1970s: inter-gang rivalries spiralled into a continuous series of violent outbursts. New policy measures were introduced, but the violence was virtually uncontrollable and the curfew was an extreme measure. It was from this conflict-riven context that there emerged a youth culture brimming with a vitality and enthusiasm for an end to violence and a greater harmony in relations between whites and blacks. 'Why must the youths fight each other?', asked the band called The Specials in their number, *Ghost Town*. This band was the vanguard of the movement called two-tone, perhaps the most impressive ethnically-integrated youth subculture in the post-war period.

The punk–rasta relationship had become unhinged by the turn of the decade. Both movements continued to attract adherents, though there were no meaningful links between them as there were in the 1970s when rastas and punks joined at clubs such as the Roxy, the Vortex (in London) and Rebecca's (in Birmingham). But cultural connections between white and black youths were enlivened by the coming of two-tone. Here was a potent unifying force that brought youths together in a social stand against racism and indeed many other reactionary elements of the 1980s.

Two-tone had unlikely origins. In 1978–9, there was a mod revival. Kids of 16 and 17 began dressing up in the garb of the mods: parkas, striped blazers, tab-collar shirts, etc. Motor scooters, decorated with multiple lamps and chromed side panels, began appearing on urban streets; 'mod sounds' discos opened. A feature movie based on the Who's album, *Quadrophenia*, which plotted the experiences of a mod youth of the 1960s, was released with some success. There was even a re-issue of Cohen's sociological study, *Folk Devils and Moral Panics!*

The revivalists looked very much like the original mods, though the music they listened to was substantially different: the sounds of the revival were basically white, mainly bands like the Small Faces and the Who, who were mod bands all right, but not the real stuff of which mod sounds were made. In fact, the whole revival had a somewhat hollow ring about it. Maybe it was a little more than a coincidence that *Quadrophenia* came out at precisely the same time as the revival because the second coming of the mods seemed to be more a product of commercial 'hype' (for hyperbole, an exaggeration) than street creativity.

Still, the importance of the mod revival for our purposes was that it prompted renewed interest in the ska and bluebeat music so popular – and, in some cases, emblematic – among the first mods. In particular, the 'Rudie' songs made a strong comeback. Rudie was a sort of a folk hero character who cropped up in song after song: *Rudie's in Love*, *A Message for Rudie*, etc. He was the prototype rude boy: an impoverished black youth, barely scraping a living through hustling and scuffling (as Jamaicans call it), getting his kicks through stealing, fighting and opposing authority at every turn. Michael Thomas described the original Jamaican rude boys as 'the hustlers and ratchet men and small-time superflies of West Kingston. They haven't been to school and they can't get a job and a lot of the time they can't is because they don't want work' (1973).

The rebellious violent image of the rude boy struck chords with the skinheads of the 1970s and rudie music was enormously popular. Many black youths were accepted by the otherwise xenophobic skins because of their connections with what was then called rock steady music (an outgrowth of bluebeat and ska and a predecessor of reggae). In a way, the rude boy lyrics captured the growing spirit of the day: dissident, angry and, sometimes, just plain aggressive.

The rude boy became a sort of generic concept, symbolizing those factions of youth alienated by the media's commercialization of punk but still retaining the vital critical impulse of the 1960s. The mod revivalists were attempting to recreate the heady, anti-authoritarian spirit of the 1960s, but were awkwardly anachronistic and more than fractionally influenced by the media hypes. Yet their importance lay in their exhumation of the rude boy figure.

At the very start of the 1980s, it was difficult if not self-defeating to try to disentangle the intermeshing complex of mod, rude boy and two-tone. Ostensibly, 'two-tone' was the name of an independent record label; it was a company started in Coventry by young people with little resources but an abundance of musical ideas. Local bands like the Specials AKA, the Selector and, from London, Madness, were the first to record on the label. The music was straight from the 1960s mod era. Madness, in fact, drew its name from a hymnal bluebeat track by the West Indian figure, Prince Buster, who attracted what some call 'cult status' amongst early mods. This band, in particular, captured the rude boy ethos. Songs were a blend of old revamped bluebeat and ska sounds with new originals incorporating rude boy lyrics; the overall effect was an almost perfectly authentic recreation of the sounds of the 1960s. The influence of punk was evident in the pronunciation of lyrics; no mimicking of American accents, but a very sharp accentuation of London or Midland dialects as if to emphasize that this was the music of the streets.

Bands, old and new, began to identify with (or, more accurately, *be* identified with) two-tone; it, as Timothy White put it, 'combined a ska revival with the antic energies of punk' (1983, p. 21). From Birmingham came the Beat, a combination of ageing West Indian musicians and white school-leavers. Already established as a musical force in the early punk days was Paul Weller's brainchild, the Jam from London; the trio dressed in mod-inspired clothes, like mohair suits and French shoes, and mixed straight love songs with clever invectives against the social order. The Jam, in general, and Weller, in particular, became the most successful products of the period, attracting mod, punk, and two-tone adherents – though, of course, there was no clear demarcation between these groups – before they broke up in late 1982.

To varying degrees, all the groups identified with two-tone were critical of aspects of society, whether it be general phenomena such as inequality, violence and unemployment or specific institutions such as marriage or mental asylums. Their followers, again to varying degrees, associated with the critiques. The single unifying bond of the whole movement was the abhorrence of racism. Two-tone was meant to convey the feeling that whites and blacks were simply two different tones of one skin colour; there was no natural break between youths, but a continuum of tones – and, at the two extremes, were white and black. Hence two-tone. Virtually all the bands had black and white members. Some, like the influential UB40, whose name was derived from the code number of the form received when registering as unemployed, had dreadlocked rasta members playing alongside neatly-groomed mod look-alikes. This band, based in the West Midlands, treated racism amongst youths as one of its central issues and used its popularity in the early 1980s as a platform for youth, often offering concert concessions for those producing evidence of their unemployment. As unemployment reached 10 per cent, UB40 sang: 'I am the one in ten, a number on a list. I am the one in ten, even though I don't exist. Nobody knows me, though I'm always there. A statistical reminder of a world that doesn't care.'

(*One in Ten*, New Claims/ATV, 1981).

Two-tone was perhaps the most invigorating movement of the early 1980s; its performers and followers were dedicated to a steadfast opposition to racism in its every manifestation and committed to encouraging more mixing and understanding between blacks and whites. Two-tone concerts were quite often more than purely musical events and were geared to political campaigns, as were the Rock Against Racism gigs of the late 1970s. In this respect, two-tone was the counter-vailing force to the other great motive power amongst youth of the 1980s – fascism (which we will come to shortly).

Two-tone concerts were events of celebration and criticism. They celebrated the unification of youth, white and black, yet criticized the growing presence of forces that threatened that unity. Its followers were a mixture of whites and blacks and, to a much more limited extent, young Asians – all dressed in a manner reminiscent of the original mods: sharply cut jackets, slim lapels, pork pie hats, narrow trousers and tennis shirts came back into vogue. Two-tone became a truly dialectical movement because its music was both *vox populi*, a reflection of the voice of the people, and a stimulus to those people. It conveyed the feelings, senti-ments and emotions of kids on the streets, yet, at the same time, translated these into coherent messages which were, in turn, picked up by those kids, thus prompting clarity of thought and maturity of perspective. The process was reciprocal and dynamic.

I might be accused of exaggerating the importance of two-tone, for, at the end of the day, like other youth subcultures, it achieved nothing tangible. But so what? It did lend form and coherence to a vague set of apprehensions about the world as it confronted many inner city youths. Not all youths were disposed to look for easy scapegoats and identify Asians or blacks as the causes of their problems; some at least were prepared to probe more deeply and locate the source of the problems at a deeper level, at the same time recognizing that hostility between whites and blacks/Asians was ultimately destructive and of no relevance to their general interests.

Some said that the end of two-tone as a distinct movement came in 1981, symbolized perhaps by the splinter of the Specials to Fun Boy Three. This three-man (two black, one white) outfit became a total commercial success and, indeed, outstripped the residual band they left behind as Specials AKA. Madness had an interesting history; in the wake of their early success they left behind an embarrassing legacy of a substantial skinhead following which obviously jarred with their two-tone devotees. The band left the 'two-tone' label and became a major commercial success with a chain of hit singles and albums. During the successful period, the band abandoned the two-tone identity and became integrated into the mainstream of popular music.

I prefer to view two-tone less as a recognizable youth movement, more as an impulse felt by certain sections of youth. If viewed in this way, two-tone's life wasn't necessarily linked to the developments of the bands. If it were, then two-tone was dead by 1981; alternatively, we can see the spirit of two-tone as living on, unattached to any particular bands, but continually being enlivened by the necessary opposition to racism. As nazism and racism spread amongst some factions of youth, then two-tone grew and remained as a countervailing tendency.

ROMANTIC INDIFFERENCE

Sandwiched in between the two extremes of two-tone and the mark two skins were groups of youth who exhibited no identifiable stance on racism or other socially significant issues. Two-tone was a genuinely collective enterprise like other youth cultures based on music, but constructed around common efforts, shared aims and perceived enemies. Of course, all youth subcultures are collective in the sense that they just can't exist without the cooperation, recognition and identification of others. You can't create a youth culture by yourself; unless others identify you as either as one of 'us' or perhaps one of 'them', then you are condemned to being an eccentric – particularly if you choose to adorn yourself with somewhat bizarre clothing. So, it would be impossible to envisage the rise of new romanticism in the 1980s without a gigantic collective effort.

The irony of it all is that the new romantics were totally and utterly committed to being unique; they went to the most extreme lengths in their strenuous efforts to be completely different. Hair was dyed in not just different, but often fluorescent, colours, sometimes in intricate patterns; it was then fashioned into petrified manes – spikes, like long icicles, jutting from the scalp. Clothes were made from outlandish fabrics and designed to project the image of exotica: hugely wide trousers, elongated jester-pointed shoes, flamboyant, frilly blouses. There was no gender differentiation for clothes; nor for the stark make-up worn to great dramatic effect by males and females.

New romanticism was the most utterly narcissistic youth subculture: its adherents were preoccupied with one thing – themselves. More accurately, the new romantics were interested in *displaying* themselves for others. It was *carte blanche* for these young peacocks. If it looked different and could attract others' attentions, then it was worn. So, men wore dresses and dropper ear-rings; women wore soldiers' uniforms, boots, etc. Literally, anything went . . .

The Blitz wine bar in London's Covent Garden is popularly taken as the first authentic haunt of new romantics. A discothèque over the bar acquired a reputation for attracting the more exotically-dressed. The clientele became known as 'blitzkids'. This was around late 1979 and, during 1980, the influence spread north. In Birmingham, for example, the Rum Runner club, previously a middle-aged club-cum-gambling-casino, underwent a transformation. Subtle dress restrictions were introduced, like 'nothing too straight'! Every patron of the new romantic clubs and discos was an example of studied desire to be different – and be recognized as such. As David Bowie, himself idolized by new romantics, characterized the movement: 'There is a grim determination to be fashionable at all cost.'

The band enthused over by new romantics reflected the effort to be extravagantly dressed. Spandau Ballet believed their appearance to be equally as important as their music to the stage act. Japan, a sort of hybrid of Bowie and Roxy Music, showed a similar concern. Other bands to capture the new romantics' imagination were Simple Minds, Kraftwerk and the pre-commercial Human League. The common factor in the 'futurist' music was the use of electronics: synthesized sound replaced the more conventional instruments to the point where some bands would simply taperecord their whole set and operate consoles on stage, virtually eliminating any need actually to play instruments 'live'. The aforementioned German band Kraftwerk took this to extremes, on occasions, substituting themselves with plastic dummies and leaving the stage completely while the taped music played.

New romanticism was totally self-indulgent, a predominantly white culture with no focus beyond the individual: the youths made a most dramatic bid to divorce themselves from the drab monotony of the working-day by escaping into an artificial fantasy world in which people dressed up as swashbuckling pirates or Rob Roy characters. Emphasis was always on appearance, form as opposed to content. There was no political edge to the movement unless you allow for the fact that dressing up as a response to everyday life may in itself be a political statement. Overtly, there were not even broad programmes. Important social matters affected the lives of young people, like the lack of work, racism, inadequate schooling. New romantics felt these, but withdrew from them, sealing themselves into a make-believe world populated by beautiful people who were similarly unconcerned by material affairs and who structured their lives around looking good and listening to music.

The other great force of political indifference of the time was, almost predictably, heavy metal, by then a dinosaur of youth culture, surviving its contemporaries and lasting seemingly without change into the 1980s. The dress remained the same, as did the political apathy and, of course, the music. HM was, by this time, a complete industry; its items ranged from full-length feature movies (about fifteen, at the time of writing) through lapel buttons and T-shirts – these mundane items providing turn-overs in the millions of pounds brackets. One of the features of heavy metal was the penchant of its devotees to collect memorabilia, particularly souvenirs of concerts, so a T-shirt bearing the legend 'Black Sabbath, 1983 Tour' would signify the follower's presence at that event.

New romanticism was not nearly as resilient as heavy metal and had exhausted itself by the end of 1981. Clothes and make-up became less bizarre, music grew less avant-garde. The new romantics, unlike heavy metal kids, had no sense of belonging to a succession of generations originating in the past and extending into the future. Like a millenarian episode, new romanticism grew out of the new spiritual crisis of youth in the early 1980s, exhibited itself in an orgiastic, ecstatic near-religiosity, then died quickly and quietly. It was a sort of celebration of contemporary decadence with males and females dressing alike, yet at the same time an expression of the anxiety of youth. The social upheavals were taking their effect on youth in the early 1980s and the future depression was unstoppable and immanent. Since society seemed to have little future, it made sense to live only for the moment, to concentrate solely on oneself, become a connoisseur of the art of self-attention.

It's facile to discard new romantics and the everlasting heavy metal kids as unimportant in the general span of post-war youth cultures. True, they were less political, less vocal and more private than many of the others. But, at another level, they were saying something significant about the passion of youths to live for themselves without worrying about the situations of others, about the development of purely personal pre-occupations and about the erosion of political awareness. We can't suggest that just because these two cultures weren't as obvious and as strident in their demands as, say, two-tone kids or punks, that they weren't conscious of the deteriorating situation in which they found themselves. I would suggest that these people too sensed the intensifying futility of trying to improve their material lives and so convinced themselves that what really mattered was that portion of their lives over which they could at least exert some control.

In this chapter, I have dealt with two basic strategies of youth reflecting a growing despair of a changing society and a broadening understanding of it. In the late 1970s and early 1980s, the sense of loss and a concern with the future were commonplace. Some groups seemed to understand it with a sociological brilliance: punks, rastas and two-toners, for example, posed trenchant critiques and, in their own sometimes eccentric ways, alternatives. New romantics and heavy metal kids continued more disguised critiques but opted for strategies or measures designed to enhance their own lives, to ensure their own health of mind as opposed to upgrading others. It was as if they could all foresee a nuclear holocaust; but while some outraged groups began marching in protest, others busied themselves building their own fragile and ultimately wasteful fall-out shelters. All were fated similarly; all their strategies suggested a widespread loss of confidence in the future.

Each youth subculture showed celebratory elements, but these belied the desperate concern for survival which gave each subculture its point. In punk, the concern was disguised as anarchy, in the new romanticism as hedonism. But for every youth touched by these movements, there was another reality – the reality of the streets. In the 1980s, racial violence in the ghettos, in the schools generated an atmosphere of chronic tension that occasionally erupted into full-scale riots. Unemployment hit the poor, the young and the blacks most severely, then spread to the middleclass, whose standards of living were systematically corroded. (The decreasing number of white-collar jobs, for example, required less skill and so conferred less security.) To this reality could be added events from far-flung corners, all of which contributed to the sense of no future: distant wars in the Middle East, uprisings in south and central America, occupations in Afghanistan and Poland, escalations of the arms race, the economic decrepitation of the West. These were small but complementary elements in the atmosphere of domestic crisis.

The modes adopted by youths to express their discontent and anxiety had the effect of actually attenuating the sense of crisis. Gone were the days when youths went through a phase of panic before settling down to mere fashion or style; gone were the simpler forms of the teds, mods and rockers. Now, there was a bewildering complex of cultures, each harbouring vague, sometimes contradictory, frequently impossible and usually bizarre aspirations. But each of the modes dealt with so far were responses to things youths felt to be wrong. Like racism, unemployment, insecurity; these were novel and growing features of the social world young people were growing up in and they were features felt to be undesirable. In a very different way, other sets of young people were reacting to elements they thought were undesirable, but for different reasons. The groups in this chapter were young and fresh enough to want to encourage change, if it was positive change. For others, the new was an abhorrence; they wanted to revert to an older, more traditional, altogether more solid way of life. And, in their way, the mark two skinheads made perhaps the single most significant impact of any post-war youth culture and most certainly captured the mood of the 1980s with an electrifying horror. We'll look at them in the next chapter.

MARK IN DC

. . . you hear a lot of bullshit about DC; what a nightmare it is and all that. But, actually it's not that bad there. Well, there's a sound bunch of guys at Nottingham; real hard geezers some of them. Good lads, mind you. It takes you a couple of weeks to adjust and get used to it, but, once you're settled in, it's not that different from life on the outside.

Look at it this way: you were doing fuck all every day in any case. So, if you do the same now, what's the difference? You can't have a drink, but neither can anybody else, so that doesn't matter much. You never enjoyed the taste of beer that much, anyway. Dressing up's another thing: you've got no clothes. But you never had any money to buy decent clothes with anyway. Still, that never stopped you as there was always ways and means of getting clobber cheap off some of the guys in town who had nicked it – or you could even did a bit of shoplifting yourself. Easy.

Women. That's another thing of course. Still, you just have to go without. Anyway, they put stuff in your tea so that you don't feel like it. Just as well really. The only women you see are your old gal and sister when they visit you. They've never got very much interesting to report about things on the outside. There is one thing about DC: they keep you occupied there. On the streets, it was all dossing, but here they make you graft – get you doing anything to keep you occupied. It's good, you suppose, being occupied all the time that is. You don't have time to get depressed, especially with the other guys who are always getting up to something or other. There are some right jokers, real good lads.

There's a lad in there who got sent down for hammering a school-kid half to death. This geezer's son had been getting battered at school by a bully kid; so the old man put out a sort of contract on him. Les – that's the guy's name – said he'd do him for twenty quid. Anyway, he found out who this bully was, waited for him after school, then followed him until he got to a quiet place. Then: whack! He's hit him across the back of his neck with a piece of rubber hose and then laid into him. The bully ended up in hospital with broken ribs, nose – fractures everywhere. But Les and the old fella got done for it. Les is an ace guy in DC; knows everyone and everything.

You've been in about three weeks when Les comes up to you and says he wants a job done. 'What sort of job?', you ask him, and he tells you that a screw wants a black kid in your dorm done over. Now, the spades aren't too bad; they smell a bit, but they hang about with each other and keep themselves to themselves. 'You can handle it, can't you?' You don't particularly feel like it, but, then again, they are spades, so it doesn't really matter – if they were white you might start asking a few questions, but, as they're black, you'll do it in any case.

'Who wants it done, though?', you ask Les. 'Just a screw who don't like niggers, that's all you need to know init?', he says. 'Anyway, what's it to you? You don't like them black bastards, do you?' Secretly, you don't mind them, but you can't tell him that, so you say straight back: 'Do I fuck!'

The thing is, if you don't do it, they'll call you a wanker and that's the worst thing that can happen to you in DC – being known as a wanker, especially by the screws who can give you a really hard time if they want to. So, you agree to do it.

Finding a couple of guys to help you is easy; a lot of them are only looking for an excuse to beat a wog up, anyway. There's only two black geezers in your dorm, so there's not going to be any trouble from the other one. The one you want is an arrogant bastard in any case – nobody likes him, except the other coons. It's about 1.00 a.m. when you decide to make your move. You creep out of bed, taking a piece of lead you've been hiding. The other two lads are tooled up as well. You shake them and the three of you make your way to the black's bunk. You don't arouse him; you just start cracking him over the head and face. He shrieks like a woman, but the screws do nothing. He tries to get out, but he's got no chance and, after about a minute – could be less – he's virtually unconscious, lying on the floor by the side of his bed.

The good thing about spades is that their bruises don't show up. What's even better is that the screws hate them so much that no one can get into trouble by giving them a spanking. In fact, in this case, the black kid who got slapped up got held responsible for causing the aggravation and he lost time for fighting. You got off with nothing. That's because the screws want to do the blacks; they'll do them up as badly as they can.

Nobody seems to mind about the incident; it seems as if it's a normal everyday thing. Even the black guys seem to accept it as inevitable; they daren't retaliate. One did once, so you heard; he ended up with a fractured skull. Nowadays, they just accept it. It's even worse for the pakis. There aren't many of them, but they really get smacked up – and they never say boo – just take their beatings.

Once you began to wonder what it must be like being a black or paki and having to take stick all the time. But you couldn't imagine it, and it was only once. Who cares? They shouldn't be here in the first place. Now that they are, they'll just have to take their medicine. It's a miniature war really.

The rest of the time in DC is pretty much run of the mill so in that respect it's exactly as life is on the outside. As it comes towards the tenth week, you begin to start thinking about what to do when you get out. This time, it's got to be different. A job would make all the difference. Maybe you weren't trying hard enough or being too choosy before. Although it still seemed tough. Anyway, it should be better by now; there's bound to be some work knocking about. It'll be different this time. It's early in 1981; you've missed Christmas, but it's the start of a new year.

You're 18, back in Birmingham, making a fresh claim at the dole office. A new year, a new attitude. The spell away hasn't done you any harm, really. It's not nearly as bad as they reckon. You hear a lot of bullshit about DC. . . .

4

SKINHEAD MENTALITY

THE SECOND COMING OF THE SKINS

One of the perplexing problems concerning youth is why do young people coming from almost identical class and family backgrounds and experiencing very similar educations respond in totally different ways to the same circumstances? In the last chapter, we looked at groups completely committed to the attack on racism, groups uninterested in such

business and others somewhere in between. Now we have to contend with youths who showed an extreme, undiluted support for racism, who backed this up with a violence that was integral to their life-style and who openly announced their sympathies with or even allegiances to reactionary political organizations such as the British Movement (BM) and the National Front (NF).

The question is as unanswerable as, say, why do some families go to Majorca for their holidays while others with the same circumstances (income, house, number of children, etc.) go to Torquay? Or even why some people take sugar with their tea, while others don't. There are answers if we had the information and patience to look for them. But we need some broad generalization to account for the different responses of youth to similar conditions. There is a very loose relationship between such factors as class, work and area, on the one hand, and cultural response patterns on the other. The story of the 'family at war' where one brother was a ted and the other a punk illustrates this.

The problem raises itself in a most difficult form when we come to the mark two skinheads. All the other modern subcultures, including two-toners, punks, new romantics, rastas, and heavy metal kids, tried symbolically to resist what they saw as integration into mainstream society. To a greater or lesser extent, they all responded to a social order they felt to be inadequate. In the case of new romantics or heavy metal kids, there was a passive adaptation; for punks and two-toners, undisciplined lashing out at abstract forces that they felt to be oppressive. Skinheads came from exactly the same kinds of backgrounds as the others, but they were different; they wanted to reclaim or at least revive the past and reassert traditional values. What's more, they had watched their aspirations progressively frustrated and so did something about it. Not content merely to shout about how diseased and rotten the system was, skins decided they needed actually to take direct action and so chose the only means they had available to them – violence, and plenty of it. Like the other subcultures, the skinhead movement was a problem-solving effort, but the skin solution was a much more final one.

The first thing to recognize is that skinheads by no means introduced regular violence to the streets. Second, they were not a bunch of lunatics performing senseless acts of violence. Marsh, in his book *Aggro* (derived from the skins' abbreviation of aggravation), presents an argument which, for all its conceptual flaws, shows convincingly that it is only the shape or style of violence among humans which changes and that the violence of skinheads is a timeless human phenomenon (1978). In the same book, Marsh chronicles the patterns of violence practised by teds, mods and rockers: 'They were *displays* of aggression and the prospect of getting seriously injured was remote' (1978, p. 92, emphasis added).

Marsh's point is that the violence amplified by the media was, prior to the over-reporting, quite 'ceremonial and constrained' and never really reached the heights of seriousness suggested. In particular, the violence of supporters on football terraces, in which skinheads in the 1970s were heavily involved, Marsh suggests, was marked by an unwritten internal regulation, captured by the title of his other book *The Rules of Disorder* (1978). As one who writes about skins, I am more easily convinced by Marsh's point than an Asian who might be the subject of one of the ritualistic attacks. Persuading someone whose head feels as if it's been hit repeatedly with a metal ball used to demolish buildings that they were simply unwilling participants in a managed ceremony or a 'display' is a job I would rather leave to Marsh.

Accepting for the moment the first point about the timelessness of violence, we can strike out the sense of novelty about the skins' aggro: there was certainly nothing new in their actions. Their choice of targets wasn't particularly fresh either as the teds of the 1950s had scapegoated blacks with some heavy intimidation. When the teds began to exploit the scapegoat potential of blacks (as a highly visible, identifiable minority) the violence took on a clear pattern. Similarly, with the mark one skinheads, the paki-bashing had ritualistic elements with the objects of violence being clearly-defined and available – often not providing too much resistance. But to reduce the whole business, as Marsh tries to do, to a ritual display, amplified, distorted, sensationalized and thereby sponsored by the media, is to take away the meaningful content of the skinheads' actions.

What I'm suggesting here is that the skins' attacks weren't simply knee-jerk responses or mimicking procedures, but conscious political acts. The mark one skinheads used what they understood to be outsiders threatening traditional ways of life as their political targets. The mark two equivalents did much the same thing, but with a difference: they broadened their scope by embracing a coherent political theory to give their actions some legitimacy. Not all skins were affiliates of the BM or NF. Indeed, Hebdige has claimed that the link between them has been exaggerated, at the same time acknowledging that: 'both skinheads and young NF supporters tend to be drawn from the same disaffected sections of the lower working class' (1981, p. 40).

Although the mark one skinheads disappeared from the scene in the early 1970s, it seems that the mentality behind the phenomenon out-lasted them. Indeed, I will argue that the skinhead mentality lives on today. The skins themselves came back into public view, boots blacked and hair cropped, in the late 1970s when they began creating disturbances at the gigs of bands such as Sham 69, Cock Sparrer and 999 – bands which were later to disavow themselves of any skinhead connections.

But it was on 3 July 1981 that the skins effectively announced their comeback. A concert at the Hambrough Tavern, Southall, London, featured the Four Skins, the Last Resort and The Business, bands which flirted with nazism and used fascist slogans in stage acts. The night before the concert a Pakistani woman and her three children were killed after their house in Walthamstow, East London, was maliciously set on fire. Incensed by this, hundreds of Asian youths converged on the concert venue where a following of skinheads had congregated. Whether or not the Asian youths initiated the fighting isn't clear, but the scene exploded – literally – when fire-bombing began and the concert hall was eventually gutted after a horrendous night of violence.

OI!

Now, the skins obviously had a solid street presence at this time, but the movements providing the political cutting edge were also making headway in the inner cities. BM and NF have histories dating back to 1919 when the Britons were established with the intention 'to protect the birthright of Britons and to eradicate Alien influences from our politics and industries' (quoted in Lebzelter, 1980, p. 41).

The Britons had a short-lived success, but the spirit generated lived on to the present day. (For detail on the development of racist parties, see Cashmore and Troyna, 1983, chapter 8.) The National Front was the result of a merger in 1967; its intention was to mount a serious political challenge. But the NF made no significant impact and failed to attract the anticipated support at general and by-elections. By 1980, it was in sharp decline and acknowledged this in its Members' Bulletin of July when it conceded that it had no hope of gaining political power 'under conditions that are stable – economically, socially and politically'. At the same time, it saw hope in a future in which 'the streets are beset by riots, when unemployment soars, and when inflation gets beyond the present degree of minimal control'.

With this in mind and with social conditions fortuitously turning in its favour, the NF began to concentrate on what Graham Murdock and Barry Troyna called 'the more immediate politics of intimidation and agitation' (1981, p. 9). Part of this was the recruitment of youth, particularly workingclass youth and the recruitment grounds were football stadia, rock concerts and inner city schools. In fact, the venture was not entirely new; in June 1977, the movement launched a youth wing, the Young National Front and published a teenage-oriented organ, *Bulldog*. It was distributed in schools along with manuals on *How to Spot a Red Teacher* and *How to Combat a Red Teacher*.

The tactics were shown to be sound by survey after survey reporting that potential support for the Front was extensive among the young. For example, research by Martin Harrop and his colleagues (1980) demonstrated that by 1977–78, over half of the NF's supporters were under 34 years old and 21 per cent were aged between 15 and 20. In its magazine, *Spearhead*, the Front confidently predicted that it would attract 'a virtual monopoly of the young vote' (May 1977).

By 1979, it was clear that the NF's existence depended on the support of the young and it found itself in a 'good news – bad news' situation. Good news: the mark two skinheads to whom racist politics had an obvious appeal were in evidence on the urban streets. Bad news: the British Movement, formed in 1968, was staging a comeback after a miserable spell in the mid-1970s and was making a strong play for the support of the young. Michael McLaughlin took over as party leader in 1975 and stimulated a rise in membership (about 3000 by 1981). Under McLaughlin, the BM, as Stan Taylor put it: 'sought to exploit the (reborn) skinhead youth culture by emphasizing sympathetic components of its own ideology, like racism and territorial exclusivity (1981, p. 539).

The complementarity between these neo-nazi groups and the skinheads couldn't have been neater. Simon Frith even went so far as to suggest that the formers' politics 'involve little more than a legitimating gloss on the skins' existing activities – defending territory, dressing in uniform, hitting strangers and women' (1981, p. 5). The general philosophy was captured by Trevor Griffiths in his play, *Oi! For England*, the title of which derives from the mark two skinheads' own brand of music called 'Oi!'. In the play, which centres around four skinheads, one of the main characters justifies his attack on an Asian:

> I'm white. I'm proud of it. I think it's the best thing ter be. . . . I ain't tekin' second place to no niggers 'n' yids in me own country.   (1982, p. 29)

This is the closest approximation to a coherent political justification for the paki-bashing episodes which became commonplace in the early 1980s and took on new dimensions in 1982 when unprovoked skinhead attacks in Coventy resulted in two Asians' deaths through stabbings. Some kind of feel for the hatred against Asians was brought out in the semi-documentary, *UndeRage* (1982) directed by Lizzie Lemon and Kim Lozinotto and filmed appropriately in Coventry. Asked if he'd ever consider killing a 'paki', the youth answers: 'I'd kill a 5-year-old paki baby if I had the chance.' It's difficult to exaggerate the intensity of the anti-Asian sentiment among large sections of workingclass youth in the early 1980s. It eclipsed the teds' 'wog-bashing' in the 1950s and the mark one skins' intimidation of 'pakis' in the 1970s. There was a deep resentment against Asians, and it reared itself in waves of ferocious attacks against Asians.

In this respect, the skins of the 1980s were at the other pole to their contemporaries who followed two-tone and sought some kind of integration, however rough-hewn, between blacks and whites. Both groups were, in their ways, distillations of the feelings and postures of youth generally, two-toners representing a liberal response to the continuing presence of racialism, skins caricaturing an older workingclass tradition. Because of this, skins were sometimes held up as exemplary citizens, as the NF publication *Nationalism Today* made clear: 'Skinheads share many of the attitudes of their parents, but with the difference that they do not have the old political loyalties of their parents and they are also willing to act.' (April 1982, p. 2).

Similarly, Hebdige saw skinheads as anachronisms, harkening back to:

A way of life, a set of values and attitudes which, according to some social historians, did not emerge until the late nineteenth century when the British Empire was at its most powerful, when imperialism, nationalism and Toryism were beginning to figure prominently in the language of the pubs and the music halls.   (1981, p. 40).

There is something compelling and insistent about this type of conservatism amongst the young. The search for change and innovation, for newness and spontaneity is best mounted from a secure base, when things seem stable and familiar so that, if all else fails, a return to a sound home, a steady job and recognizable surroundings is possible. It's more easily aborted when insecurity, instability and unpredictability abound. Then conservatism or even retrogression takes grip. The tendencies to fascism in the depressed 1930s highlight the relationship between social upheaval and extreme, fanatical conservatism.

The skinhead rebirth of the 1980s was not a confident attempt of high-morale youth striding forth ambitiously. It was a desperate longing of young people scrambling for a vision of hope and finding only a flawed, misleading but persuasively simple ideology based on some mystical concept of a solidly traditional white workingclass community, prosperous and untainted by the evils of outside invaders. The skinheads felt worthless themselves and, in a sense, they were right; the feelings bit deeply into their self-esteem and resurfaced as a despairing kind of violence and racialism. Their sense of purpose gone, they looked for some kind of guiding force and found it in an extreme, loose philosophy and a racist idealism. But the impulse behind the movement to the political right was a strong one and one which gained momentum as more and more disaffected young people discovered some sense of friction, albeit a destructive one, in right-wing racialism.

HARDNESS

The BM/NF image dovetailed beautifully with the hardness so integral to much workingclass life. Violence has always been a resource for people who have no other means of acquiring status or prestige. If you've got money or come from a good family, you can afford to look well, go to the right places, travel in style. If you've got nothing and have little chance of getting anything in the future, then you have to devise other ways of climbing the social scale. One way is quite literally to fight your way up it. Being hard is a valuable possession in itself: it commands the respect of others, even if it's a grudging respect, and so gives the harder person an edge in the social hierarchy. Coming from workingclass backgrounds, the youths who became attracted by the NF/BM skinhead liaison were invariably those who had proved, or at least tried to prove, themselves as hard men. The tattoos that adorned their bodies were not so much for decorative purposes as a statement that the individual had withstood the pain of having a needle continually jabbed into him. The blue spot marked indelibly on the left facial cheek was a proud symbol of the youth's having toughened up with a spell in Borstal (even some of those who hadn't been in a Borstal marked their cheeks).

Hardness was an essential attribute of the skins because the violence was so much a part of their philosophy. It wasn't enough speculating about the deterioration of society and its invasion by unwanted outside agents; direct action had to be taken and violence was that action.

The rallies, the breaking-up of left-wing group meetings, the disruption of two-tone concerts were ideal for the confluence of the skins and the NF/BM (one of the prominent two-tone bands, the Specials, was forced to stop touring because of the continual havoc caused by skins at concerts). Such events lent themselves perfectly to the brand of direct action craved by the skins and encouraged by the political groups. They could demonstrate their hardness and, at the same time, displace some of their anger on groups they despised, such as the Anti-Nazi League organization.

Everything the skins stood for contrasted with two-tone, yet it was they who brought the greater force to the UK's youth. They did so because they reflected more accurately the society of which they were part. Garry Bushell, a rock journalist, reckoned Oi! was a form of 'populist punk, raucous and rowdy and workingclass . . . the culture of youth on society's scrapheap' (in *Contemporary Affairs Briefing*, August 1981, p. 1).

Perhaps the skinhead movement was a 'populist punk', a force giving firm contours and sharp edges to the anarchic, nihilistic energies of the late 1970s. It provided some kind of vision for an otherwise chaotic bundle of criticisms against society. On the other hand, it brought to the surface many of the features integral to society.

For instance, the skins were aggressively masculine, relegating women to the ranks of servants. As one skin told me: 'I'm not saying we don't respect women; I mean I like my bird to stick up for me and she does, she'll have a fight as hard as any geezer. But it stands to sense, they can't be the man's equal can they? I've got to be the gaffer; I wouldn't be a man otherwise. The man's gotta be the gaffer.' They were town chauvinists to an almost absurd degree; as some Sunderland skins replied when asked by Jeremy Seabrook 'Who's your own people then?' 'British.' 'English. I hate people from Scotland.' 'Scotland! I hate 'em from Newcastle' (1982, p. 116). And of course, they were savagely racist, a fact encapsulated by a skin who reasoned: 'If you're white, you want to live with other whites, right? There ain't any way the races can mix together. It's only natural that can't work. It's been proved. The only way whites can get off their knees is to get rid of all the pakis, blacks and the rest of 'em and make the white race pure – pure white.' Reminiscent of the Britons – amongst others?

As 1982 ticked by, the skinhead appearance grew less prevalent. The green combat jackets, short narrow trousers and military paratrooper boots which replaced Doctor Martens stayed in evidence, but the numbers of skinheads got smaller and hair got longer – not much longer, mind. As a recognizable subculture, the skinhead movement lost its force by 1983: its decline paralleled that of its political counterparts, the BM and NF, and many skins grew weary of the lack of political success. Like John, who in 1982 said: 'I used to go to all the NF meetings in the room over the Oak (a pub). I was a dead regular, went to the rallies, the lot . . . but, I think it's gone now. The Front doesn't seem to make any headway at all. I know it's like leaving the sinking ship, but there's no point any more. The Front can't get anywhere.'

Another kind of response was that the skins had merely used the political organizations 'for the crack', or action, and just lost interest after a year or so. It was a less prevalent view, but an interesting one articulated by ex-skin Jimmy: 'I only used to go for the crack. It was sommat to do going to the meetings and giving it the old Sieg Heil and all that caper. I enjoyed it. The knocks (fights) we had were fucking terrific. I can't honestly say I was into the politics of it though; it was more good fun than anything else. I didn't understand the other stuff about the Jews and that; I just wanted to get into a few bust-ups and kick some paki's head in.'

When the BM and NF fell short of expectations and the kicking ceased to be fun, the liaison became unglued, though, in many urban parts skinheads retained their affiliations into the 1980s. For the most part, however, the skinheads dropped from public view and became known as a relatively benign force, a striking contrast to their heady days as folk devils.

But the skinheads' story doesn't just end with their disappearance from the streets of the inner cities. Despite the fading of the political alignment, it could be argued that the skins remained unshaken. Their hair might have grown longer and their shouts of 'Sieg Heil' quieter, but the basic mentality informing the skinhead response persisted. To push the point further, I could suggest that the same mentality behind the mark one skins was kept going by the less celebrated 'suedeheads' who arrived in their wake and sustained by various disaffected groups of urban youths who felt predisposed towards the types of racism and cultural conservatism favoured by the early skins. The same mentality was given momentum by the steeply declining conditions workingclass youth found themselves in at the end of the 1970s and provided with political dimensions by the neo-nazi parties that capitalized on the collapse of the age of affluence and the crisis brought about by unemployment and inflation.

'The right-wing backlash' is the term usually applied to the reaction of ultra-conservative groups sensing a deterioration following a period of social change amidst relative prosperity. Typically, the call is to restore conditions to some state of stability and the tactic is to promote the image of a pure and glorious golden age – usually based on some spurious history. The expulsion or even extermination of contaminating elements is a common strategy employed by fascist groups; for example, German Nazis made Jews their targets, as the American Ku Klux Klan made blacks theirs. Such scapegoating is an obvious and, often, an effective manoeuvre, as it was in the UK at the end of the 1970s. But, as the social problems besetting youth continued into the 1980s, the racism associated with scapegoating also continued and sustained credibility amongst many quarters.

The skinhead mentality was and, indeed, is an enduring one: inner-city youths may have drifted away from the Front and the British Movement, but the state of mind that facilitated the allegiance in the first place has stayed and is being transmitted down the age groups. So that, in 1983, a 14-year-old schoolboy was able to tell me: 'I don't get on with the blacks and pakis at school. I don't want to 'cause I don't like 'em and I want to see 'em sent back to where they come from.' It seems a malicious, but familiar, comment from one so young, but it's representative of many school-kids. 'Niggers' and 'Nig-nogs' are words which appear regularly in the vocabularies of white workingclass youth.

Mark, whose career I've been tracking, was typical of the skinhead mentality. A former skin himself, he was peripherally involved with the BM, then grew disenchanted: 'I thought all this Sieg Heil business was a load of bollocks, really. It was a laugh to start with, but I never took it seriously like some of the others. Then I just sort of stopped going to the meetings and that.'

But, hang on, Mark: does that mean you had a change of heart and repaired your old ways? 'Does it fuck! I still want the coons and pakis out. They're taking the country over the way we're going. I suppose the British Movement are right . . . and I agree with most of what they're saying about the wogs. I just got pissed off with going . . . That doesn't mean I wouldn't smash some fucking paki's face in, though.'

Another ex-skin, 'Rat' (to his mates) had also been involved with both the BM and the Front before falling away. Like Mark, his teen years had been punctuated with spells in various institutions. Scarred all over his body – 'I've had 26 stiches in all' – he worked as a trainee engineer after leaving school with few qualifications, then got made redundant and had only one other job (in a bacon-packing factory) in the next four years. 'Assault, wounding, burglary and that sort of thing', was how he described his offences. 'But I wouldn't do it to old ladies or anything like that: only other guys.' And one group in particular: 'Oh pakis! I don't like them; I've never spoken to one at all. I'd do one of them for nothing.'

He provided a retrospective view on the skinhead subculture: 'It was great a few years ago, fights all the time, rallies, Front marches and that caper. But it's died off a bit now and the skins about at the moment are little kids really; they don't know what it's all about. When we were strong, though, it was different. . . . I think the skins had the right idea. It's still there, the mood, I mean; but, you know you don't see that many (skins) about 'cause they're sick of getting singled out by the old bill all the time. They (police) think, "Oh there's a skinhead; we'll nick him for something or other."'

Like many other panic-emitting subcultures, the skinheads had to face the wrath of society's forces of control. Folk devils are invariably brought to the attention of the courts and duly dealt with and skinheads were subjected to the treatment. But, it didn't totally suppress the dynamic or inner motor of the skinhead response and, in 1983, senior skins were still prevalent. Like Stewart, who described himself as a 'grown-up skin' who at 20 had become disenchanted with both the skinhead movement and their political wings. His reasons were rather interesting too: 'I used to get into trouble all the time; I did time in Borstal for cutting a guy up. But it gets too much so I don't bother now. I've grown my hair a bit now. I used to be a skinhead and I was in the British Movement. We used to meet in an Erdington pub. But I saw one or two black guys there. So I couldn't figure that out. But, I thought, well, if we're against them and they're going to the same meetings we do, what the hell is going on? So I stopped going and lost a bit of interest in skins.'

Although a very small minority, there were a number of black skinheads in the 1980s, presumably drawn to the movement by their peers. Growing up in the inner city estates often means forced associations with people who may be neither sympathetic with your situation or receptive to your views. Black and white youths grow up together, experiencing similar, but not the same conditions. The main difference is, of course, the blacks are constantly reminded of their blackness, particularly when they go for jobs. Blackness does make a difference and black youths are sharply aware of that fact. Hence many of them, like rastas, cultivate distinctly black subcultures. Others may hold a similarly clear conception of the unique problems linked to blackness, yet choose not to reflect on them. Let me chronicle the fact that some black youths, far from being antagonistic towards or just indifferent about skins, actually feel strongly for their cause and involve themselves with skinhead activities, like attending BM meetings. Eddie was one such affiliate: 'I get on with white guys better than I do blacks. Most of my mates where I live are white, most were into the skinheads and I can see that 'cause there are too many blacks in this country; and everybody knows the pakis are gonna take over the country the way things are going. They've got loads of money and own big businesses and things. I get on with white mates, but I hate pakis.'

The skinheads had their fair share of enemies, particularly in the form of the Anti-Nazi League and vigilante groups who patrolled housing estates to protect residents. Skins also spurred resistance gangs from Asian youths, tired of being subjected to beating. Gangs like the 'redheads' (because they dyed their hair with henna colouring) were made up of young workingclass Asians who had taken as much stick as they could stand off the skins. The image of Asian youth as rather passive characters interested only in furthering their academic careers took a few knocks in the 1980s. They showed quite vividly that, when prompted, they could mobilize for action with chilling effectiveness, as they did at Southall. Periodically, Asian youth has become a violent force when confronted by the skinhead threat.

The skinhead appearance may disappear; the skinhead outlook will not. So long as conditions are conducive to scapegoating, the idea that specific groups are to blame for gross social changes will persist. Directing violence at recognizable groups is a way of getting rid of frustrations and anxieties that may be unconnected with those groups. In this sense, scapegoating works well and will continue to do so for as long as the lives of workingclass kids are made sufficiently intolerable that they have to look for reasons. They ask: 'Why is it that I'm always poor and can't seem to make any headway?' The answer, albeit a wrong one, unfolds and they react on the basis of it.

But, while the skinhead mentality remains, other forms of venting frustration will surface. An indication of what those other forms might take came in the summer of 1981, when gangs of urban youths were stirred into mass action. Many explanations of the causes of the 1981 riots were offered; my version follows in the next chapter.

MARK
SIEG HEIL

. . . you feel great when you get out of the barber's shop. You run the palm of your hand across the bristly stumps on your head. Most of your mates are into the skinhead revival, they're having their hair cropped and getting the gear. You buy a really smart green combat jacket with the first week's money you get off the dole after you come out of DC.

Dave's got APL tattooed on his arm. It stands for Anti-Paki League, and it means simply that you hate pakis. He's got all the gear now, boots and everything. Everybody seemed to hate pakis when you were younger, but now there's a way to show it; it's like the new skinhead stuff is a uniform, it shows you belong to an army of people who want certain things. Army is a good word 'cause it means that you're all together, united, fighting as a unit against the enemy. The enemy in this case is easy to spot.

The new skins are better organized than the old ones and this is 'cause they're more political. It's good to have somebody to teach you things about the world and get you into shape, like the real army. Now there's parties like the National Front and the British Movement and they've got the same views as the skins. A load of your mates are getting involved with them, so you're interested. The BM have got loads of skins in them. No wonder: they're always handing out leaflets at the football matches and at concerts. A lot of what they've got to say makes sense. Like they reckon the British society's on the verge of collapsing because of the 'alien' influences; they say that it's our duty as white citizens to make a stand. They tell you that you've got to breathe new life into the 'traditional Aryan values' – that's what Hitler and his mob were trying to do. Well, let's put it this way: life hasn't been too good to you so far: no money, no job, been locked up for beating up pakis. There must be something wrong with the system 'cause the blacks can live all right on social security and the pakis have got their own businesses and all you do is struggle. The BM has got a point.

Anyway, you decide to go to a few of their meetings. They're quite good with about thirty or forty other skins there. They're held over a pub and the gaffer of the pub himself is one of the area's organizers. At the meetings they talk as if you're in the army and there's a war about to begin. You didn't realize just how bad things were getting till you listened to the speakers. The main leader is a guy called Burns, a big geezer, over fifteen stones; he shouts when he speaks, but it makes sense. 'It's not just the black scum', he says. 'We've got to destroy the reds.' It makes you think. Everybody knows that blacks are bringing the country down, but, now you see how the communists are just as bad. They're on the same side as the blacks, anyway. Everything fits into place when the speaker starts going on about Jews, as well. They've got all the money and they're trying to keep it by whatever means they can. They're cunning bastards, keeping their own race pure while others, the blacks and pakis, mix with us Anglo-Saxons and drag us down to their level. 'White power', Burns shouts at the end. Then he raises a clenched fist: 'Sieg Heil'. We all join him: 'Sieg Heil, Sieg Heil, Sieg Heil!'

The marches are good. There are hundreds of you and your mates along with the BM organizers, all marching along like a well-groomed army, chanting all the slogans, especially 'Sieg Heil'. The atmosphere is different from anything you've ever experienced. It's like everybody is three or four times as strong as they usually are; confidence is growing as the chanting gets louder. 'Kill the commies, the niggers, the yids!' are the kinds of things. It's only right though, isn't it?

Smashing up concerts is good. One night, in particular, you and a bunch of mates go along to Barbarella's club. Sham 69 are on. You only let them do two numbers. First it was gobbing at 'em, then a few of you started spitting mouthfuls of beer, then just throwing the beer – with the glass still round it. One of their roadies, a big fat guy with a skin haircut, comes lunging out and dives head first into the crowd. He cops a few of you, but everybody goes for him and starts kicking shit out of him. A load more geezers come out to help him and your lads jump up on the stage. The bouncers get stuck in and the whole thing blows up. Iron bars and sticks are coming out and glasses are being smashed everywhere. Nobody quite knew why it started, but it was good for the crack. Eventually, the old bill arrived and broke it up. But one or two of the lads managed to bust some of the coppers in the face.

You got out of that without getting nicked. In future, you won't be so lucky; in fact, you'll end up doing another three months for fighting – in a pub this time.

Around Small Heath, there's loads of pakis; but there's also a lot of skins. One night, this paki gets done over really bad. You didn't do it, but you know who did – hard bastards. Well, the pakis don't usually fight back very much, but, about two weeks after the beating-up, a big mob of about twenty or thirty of them start roaming the streets and beating up white kids. They're tooled up as well, iron bars, chains, some of them even had cutlasses. Nobody knows how many kids they did over in that one night, but it must have been quite a few 'cause everybody was talking about it the following day and about six of your lads ended up in the general hospital. The story that goes round is that these pakis have organized themselves into a team and call themselves the redheads.

The thing is: nobody knows where this mob hangs out, or even who's in them. So, the only thing you've got to do is go through the streets and do every paki you see. You've got to do it. Two nights after the beatings-up, you and about eight others go on the rampage. Every paki you see gets it. No mercy spared: they just get a good kicking and left in the street. It's exciting doing it and it makes you feel good. Well, it's only fair. If they can do some of your mates, then you've got to pay them back. They probably all know each other.

What's more, you know what you're doing is right. The police, the politicians and everybody else might have swallowed all the nonsense about racial harmony and that bollocks. But, if they'd have taken the trouble to listen to people like the BM, they might see some sense. These people have got to be kept in their place. Better still, they've got to be killed off. You've got to stop talking about how to get the country off its knees and do something about it. At least, you're putting your beliefs into practice. Anyway, it's good for the crack. . . .

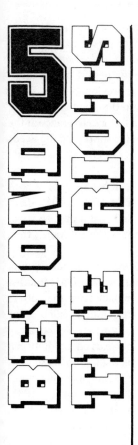

THE LUXURY GAP

Any account of youth and the cultural forms it's taken since the war breaks easily into phases. Youth in the 1950s and 1960s was liberating, exhilarating and dramatically different: the advent of rock music and its playfully rebellious overtones, the emergence of peculiar styles that young people created as symbolic of an elective identity quite distinct and separate, they thought, from the rest of society. Young people discovered that the period immediately after leaving school did not have to be merely an apprenticeship to the drudgery of a working life just like mum's and dad's. Youth was created as a special preserve, something to be celebrated and enjoyed rather than toiled at.

Older people were, at first, shocked into panic, then became resigned and then even reflected on the emancipatory effect that the new developments were having. 'The swinging sixties', as they were called were times of great liberation when new fields of self-expression were opened up and thoroughly explored by a willing new generation constructing new standards and seeking new principles.

The children born in that period of affluence and optimism are now in their late teens or very early twenties. They were born into an expectant society in which horizons were expanding, opportunities were multiplying and prospects seemed limitless.

But few things last and, as the 1960s drew to a close, so did the expectation of a beautiful future. The freedom so closely linked with the period seemed to contract and the hippies' last desperate attempt to detach themselves from society and develop an alternative based on libertarian principles was a kind of harbinger of the end of a short but important era.

It's sometimes easy to romanticize the period by pointing to the excesses of youth, the new-found freedom, the cultural innovations, the rebellious spirit and so. But, as I've stressed before, the whole enterprise was abetted by the rise of an entire section of industry responding to the demands and creating new demands of youth. Seabrook saw the period in this light: 'Of course, it was really about selling things to the previously poor. What happened was that the working class were delivered to the marketplace, not as labour, but as consumers. And it did seem like a deliverance at the time: the market seemed the perfect mechanism for supplying the needs of those with money to spend for the first time.' (*The Guardian*, 20 July 1981).

A similarly sobre view comes from Frith who, in his analysis of rock music, stated bluntly: 'Rock is a capitalist industry' (1978, p. 204). Frith argued that if young consumers 'can be persuaded that a precise style, genre, artist or image meets their needs, expresses the solution', then 'their exploitation is facilitated' (1978, p. 208).

The point is that youth is built up around the concerns of young people, but it is also built up inside the framework of a capitalist industry. Even those subcultures that seem to emanate from the gutters may be deceptive as Cohen detects: 'I am not aware of much evidence, for example, that the major components in punk originated too far away from that distinctive London cultural monopoly carved up between commercial entrepreneurs and the lumpen intellectuals from art schools and rock journals.' (1980, p. xii). Anne Campbell puts a similar point simply: 'Even anarchy can be packaged and sold by a capitalist.' (1981, p. 120). This is the idea informing Joe Jackson's number, *I'm the Man*, which tells of a sort of conspiracy in which all the subcultures and fashions attributed to youth's creativity are the artefacts of one single, scheming entrepreneur, 'the man who gave you the yo-yo'.

This less visible dimension of youth is one which can't be ignored if we're to gain an understanding of the changes occurring within youth in the 1980s. It is not just about stylistic innovation, but about the manufacture of needs – consumerism. Youth was constructed on a solid foundation of spending power, and that power has been drained. Spending has, over the past thirty years, become an integral part of youth; the products available like records, concerts, fashion clothes, are not merely functional items, but have great symbolic value; they express the persons' view of themselves. So, take the ability to buy those consumables away and it will have consequences on the sense of identity as well as the appearance.

In previous times, the most relevant question you could ask someone was: what do you do? After the creation of youth, it became almost as meaningful to ask: what kind of music do you like? Are you a mod or a rocker? Patterns of consumption were virtual determinants of identity;

looking the part was being the part. Consumer items bit deeply into areas of human experience. +

But consumerism did not only affect the young. They were the banner-bearers of the new age of affluence, but the workingclass generally benefited. Supermarkets brought a seemingly limitless range of goods to shoppers; convenience foods, washing machines and dish-washers released women from unnecessary chores; the expansion of a new entertainments industry provided new areas of diversion in leisure hours. Middleclass life-styles were suddenly in reach of ordinary workingclass families and the process of *embourgeoisement* went into operation.

At the same time, there was, as I've noted before, a disintegration of the traditional workingclass community. The neighbourhood was split asunder as post-war urban redevelopments began and old kinship ties and associations broke apart. New houses replete with 'all mod cons' sprang up in the suburbs and high-rise estates in the inner cities. Refrigerators, hi-fi equipment and, inevitably, televisions were packed into them. The nostalgia prompted by the break-up of the old community was felt by the older workingclass; later it was to be redefined as a basis for action by the mark one skinheads.

The children who were to become the youth of the 1980s grew up in this atmosphere of consumerism. They were reared on supermarket food and educated on television advertisements exhorting them to buy new products. At this stage, the money was available, thanks to the relative prosperity high employment brings. Kids wanted the goods the ads told them to want and parents, buoyed up by the state of the economy, saw that they were provided for.

But when the affluence of the 1950s and 1960s waned and the decline of the 1970s began, the market and the consumers got out of sync and the demands of the teenage population stopped being met. The effects were not felt evenly, of course; those poorest sections of society were affected most seriously, having had their needs steadily boosted by ads and their wants stimulated by the desire to keep up with the proverbial Joneses.

Changes in industry accompanied this immiserization. Automation made crafts and trades redundant and activated the need for a new type of worker to operate machines. The movement away from primary produc-tion, such as in mines, factories and mills, further agitated traditional patterns of work. So the working population had to undergo another upheaval because its sense of having labour to offer and bargain with was corroded by these changes. Rising unemployment and the concomitant loss of buying power and the changing occupational structure of industry damaged the workingclass's self-evaluation.

But the youth of the 1980s knew nothing of this devaluing for, unlike their parents, they were rarely given the opportunity of experiencing what it's like to feel wanted in the first place. They knew nothing about job satisfaction, less still about meaningful employment. Productive contributions were never demanded of them; they were simply motivated to consume, brought up to respect the power of money and what it can buy – contentment, material comfort, happiness, etc. Since youth first appeared in the 1950s, the appetites of the young have been whetted by a section of industry, but they have not been taught about the counterpart to consumption: production. Social changes ensured that work for the majority of the young was going to be mechanical or meaningless anyway. So when unemployment rendered most of them superfluous, it was not such a dramatic loss. Significant, however, was the discrepancy opened up by, on the one hand, being psyched up to be consumers and, on the other, being denied the resources necessary to consume. That discrepancy was captured by the northern band Heaven 17 whose 1983 album bore the name *The Luxury Gap*.

THE TANTALOS SYNDROME

Tantalos was a mythological Greek king who was condemned to stand in the abyss of Tartarus surrounded by fruit and water which he craved but could not reach. Similarly, youths find themselves in a position in which they are shown goods, yet denied access to them; like the Greek king, they are tantalized by things that are out of their reach.

Interesting in this context is a theory first put forward by the sociologist Robert Merton who set out: 'to discover how some social structures exert a definite pressure upon certain persons in the society to engage in non-conforming rather than conforming conduct' (1969, p. 255). The theory stated that the 'pressure' takes the form of a great emphasis on the successful attainment of cultural goals. Looking at American society, Merton concluded that the ultimate cultural goal was material success which was to be conspicuously displayed. The ability to consume, therefore, was highly valued and people were encouraged, through various media such as schools and advertising, to maximize this ability – within certain boundaries.

Merton's view was that the boundaries defined the legitimate means through which people could realize their goals: in any society there are moral guidelines, or norms, to remind people of the correct way to approach their goals. Hard work, taking risks, acting on initiatives, for example, are legitimately within the boundaries.

Now, certain groups are well-equipped to achieve the goals through legitimate means; for example, those with enough wealth and power to transfer to their offspring and give them 'a start in life'. At the other extreme, there are those groups that have Sisyphean tasks to realize their goals, tasks which are made impossible under certain social conditions such as severe recessions. In these circumstances, there occurs, according to Merton, a situation of anomie, meaning that people still strive for the goals of material success, but simply don't have the opportunities to reach them through legitimate methods. So people have to devise ways of adapting to this gap between what they expect and want from society (the goals) and the opportunities they have available to get them.

Merton theorized five possible ways: (i) conformity, simply accepting the goals and the means; (ii) innovation, carrying on chasing the goals, while devising new methods of getting them, such as through crime; (iii) ritualism, abandoning the goals but rigidly going through the motions in sticking to the means of achieving them; (iv) retreatism, ditching both the goals and the means (like quitting a job and 'dropping out' of society); (v) rebellion, formulating both new goals and means.

The relevance of the theory to modern youth is apparent if we consider that the young people growing up through the 1960s and 1970s were nourished on a staple diet of TV ads and exhortations to possess products. Possession of stylish clothes, new records, stereo equipment, motor vehicles and so on was the cultural goal; and the means to get them were simply working, earning and spending. Unemployment introduced a disjuncture between the cultural goal of consumption and the opportunity channels through which the goal can be achieved. A state of anomie results. This is exactly what happened to youth in the 1980s. The motivations of young workingclass people, who are those most subjected to the 'pressure', emerge out of the frustration of deprivation after internalizing or accepting goals which can't be achieved. Hence the Tantalos syndrome.

Just how anomic youths respond to the disjuncture we began to see in 1981 when rioting broke out in virtually every inner city in the UK. In chapter 4, I described the incident in Southall in July 1981 when Asian youths clashed with skinheads. The weeks either side of the episode were packed with events which made 1981 something of a watershed in the history of youth. In the previous year, there had been a serious disturbance in the St Paul's district of Bristol after police had entered a café used mainly by blacks. A crowd assailed the police, who were eventually forced to withdraw, leaving the district a virtual 'no-go area' for some four hours. is event presaged a larger and more dramatic sequence twelve months later.

BRIXTON AND AFTER

Swamp 81 was the code name of a saturation policing operation conducted in the south London area of Brixton, which housed a large black population. As a result of the operation, a total of 1000 people were stopped and 100 arrested in four days. This aggravated what was already a tense relationship between police and locals, and it needed only an incident involving a certain Michael Bailey and a group of police officers trying to apprehend him to ignite what turned into a literally explosive scene. This particular confrontation acted as a kind of catalyst for, in its immediate aftermath, sporadic fighting escalated into a sequence of petrol bomb attacks on police vehicles and buildings. For two solid days, a three-mile area around Brixton was ringed by 1000 police with a further 3000 on call. 'Burnin' and lootin'' went on, residents smashing open shops and helping themselves to whatever goods they wanted. The cost of the damage and loss of goods was estimated in millions of pounds.

The Brixton riot, as it came to be called, involved mainly black youths in confrontation with white police. In this respect it resembled a smaller-scale version of the disorders in the Watts district of Los Angeles in the mid-1960s. As Brixton subsided, however, fighting erupted in cities across the country, this time with white youths joining blacks in an orgiastic sequence of violent destruction. The youths attacked police, property – anything they could reach. Shopping precincts were devastated, shops themselves were plundered, houses were destroyed, cars were set aflame as the national rampage continued. It was as if young people were venting the frustrations of years, though many commentators tried to deny this by depicting the riots as simply 'copycat' phenomena with the youths mimicking the events at Brixton rather than articulating protest against the conditions they found themselves in.

This wasn't a wholly satisfactory argument and it tended to mask the underlying social causes by suggesting the other episodes were only imitative exercises. Even the rather limited Scarman inquiry on Brixton acknowledged: 'The common strands in many of the major disorders, for which there is much evidence, are to be found in shared social conditions, in economic insecurity and perceived deprivation in enforced idleness because of unemployment, and in the hostility of at least a section of young people to the police.' (1981, p. 14).

'Shared social conditions' is the key here: conditions common to both black and white workingclass youths. True, blacks were disproportionately hit by feelings of economic insecurity and the 'enforced idleness' unemployment brings and we have evidence also to indicate that police practices do not always work in the best interests of blacks (IRR, 1981). Young blacks have had disruptions in their lives and, as Jeremy Seabrook emphasizes: 'Theirs has been a long experience of historical dislocation, a story of driven restlessness and uprooting. They have far less securely anchored resources with which to resist the continuing epic of dispossession to which they are heirs.' (1983, p. 63). But young whites also are affected appreciably by some of these conditions. The so-called copycat riots which climaxed on 11–12 July, involved substantial numbers of white youths and the arrest statistics reflected this (of the 3074 people arrested, 2400 were white, according to the Home Office).

Brixton and Bristol appeared to be about racism: they involved mainly young blacks in confrontation with the front-line enforcers of the system called Babylon. But it wasn't just a case of blacks vigorously protesting against police malpractice or the refusal of police to protect blacks from racialist attacks and the tendency to subject blacks to harassment. In both episodes, conflicts with the police precipitated the more serious disturbances. The same happened in Watts', Los Angeles, in 1965 when blacks took to the streets and rampaged for almost a week. But in all cases, the blacks' rage wasn't so much against the predominantly white police officers as against the system they personified. Black youths burned the houses they lived in, the shops they bought from; they destroyed the environment they lived in. And, significantly, they attacked the people they regarded as their controllers.

Perhaps these didn't seem very rational, intelligible actions, but the targets of the blacks' attacks were symbols. They were symbols of the exploitative system of Babylon. So blacks burnt and looted the actual community in which they lived, a community which stood as a testament to the impoverishment of their lives.

So the first episodes were fired by, amongst other things, blacks' feeling that their chances of improvement were cripplingly restricted by their blackness. The youths saw no point in trying to get ahead and pursue success, so turned to new ideals and unconventional ways of pursuing them. In this way, the black rioters would slot into Merton's category of rebellion; they were rebels. But, in the copycat riots, both black and white youths seemed to run amok, aimlessly destroying anything that lay in their way and wreaking havoc wherever possible. The whites weren't rioting against racialism, so what were they rioting about?

They were making a gesture, however unwittingly, against their inability to grasp the things they had been brought up to depend on, things that they used as markers for their self-identities. Their violence had its origins in a society which geared this generation to strive for and expect material benefits, then placed insurmountable barriers in their way; it stimulated their appetites, then took away the food. The result was a type of anomie and the response was to burn and loot. Simon Field, commenting on the rioting, put it like this: 'It has occurred because certain groups have lost faith in the capacity and will of establishment institutions to take their interests into account and to provide them with the means of achieving social acceptance and material success.' (1982, p. 33).

The 1981 riots saw a monumental assemblage of frustrated expectations with youths, black and white, uniting to express their basic acceptance of culturally prescribed goals and their rejection of the legitimate means to attain them – what Merton called innovation. That's precisely what burnin' and lootin' is, after all.

Subcultural differences were superseded as punk, skin and every other style enjoined in the rioting. John Ashton called the mode through which the action was organized 'spontaneous intelligence networks' (1983, p. 110). It was as if the divisions, whether based on colour, posture or sheer style, were dismissed as trivial or at least temporarily suppressed as the more urgent issue of sharing conditions and destinies became the basis for action. The frustration gave way to aggression, aggression against a system which was priming ambitions and spoiling their fulfilment.

In real terms, the 1981 riots didn't achieve much. They prompted great debate, stimulated awareness of the problems faced by unemployed (and, therefore, poor) youth, particularly the black ones and provoked the government into ordering a full-scale inquiry. Yet, in the twelve months following, no tangible improvements had been effected. If anything, there was a deterioration because another round of school-leavers joined the dole queues, thus increasing the already intense competition for jobs. But after all the explanations had been offered for the riots, it might be asked of the youths involved, 'What was the advantage in not rioting?'

In the same twelve months, there were other interesting developments which suggested that the actual experience of rioting had made some sort of impact on workingclass youth. Let me express it through the words of Dean, who'd been involved in the riots and reflected on them: 'It might have looked as if we were in it for a laugh, but there was this incredible feeling. We weren't fighting each other; like we weren't fighting the pakis or the blackies, 'cause they were with us doing the rioting. We were all fighting something else.'

Howard Tumber got similar types of responses when he investigated the influence of the media on the riots: 'We're fighting for our rights – against the police – it's not copycat' (1982, p. 12). Tumber's general conclusion was that the television had only a minimal effect on the riots. (Another report by Peter Southgate reached broadly the same conclusions, though the circulation of rumours was, he contended, important in getting youths ready to riot; 1982, p. 53).

Young people stopped fighting each other because of their colour or affiliation and fought for themselves. The process had a unifying effect on them and brought them together in a common effort. They were, as Ashton put it, 'united in a common sense of betrayal' (1983, p. 110).

Whether this had any genuine lasting impact is debatable, but certainly there were discernible changes in the general pattern of youth culture in the years that followed. For example, there was a pronounced blurring of the demarcation lines between subcultures. Not simply in uniforms, but in attitudes and postures. It became commonplace to see skinheads dyeing their hair vivid colours and shearing it into a Mohican crop or an exaggerated mane like the punks. They might also wear nose studs or earrings. Yet they'd keep the boots and half-mast jeans and still identify themselves as skins. There was a kind of cultural permutation with youths selecting items and rearranging them to produce new stylistic configurations which flew in the face of fashion.

The extremities of postures towards blacks closed up: some skins, like Malcolm, would dissociate themselves from right-wing politics: 'They (the BM/NF acolytes) have got the skins a bad name; we're not all into that; I get on great with my black mates and I know some pakis too.' A group called Skins Against Nazis emerged; punks wore swastikas. Two-tone lost its shape as an identifiable subculture and its force was dissipated. Heavy metal steamed on unaffected by the changes occurring around it. And new romanticism metamorphosed into urban vagrancy.

This urban vagrancy was an interesting phenomenon in that it seemed to parody the mood of the times. Its image conjured up what Angela Carter called 'the aesthetic of poverty that has been operating strongly at street level since the punk styles of the mid-seventies' (1983, p. 65). The style was asexually shapeless: loose trousers, sagging socks, scarves wrapped untidily around the head like a bandage beneath floppy felt hats. It was a look epitomized by the band Culture Club which became a commercial success in late 1982. The singer Boy George's dubious sexual origins suited the image perfectly: males and females dressed just the same.

The look of the disorderly vagabond radiated poverty, though, ironically, only those with substantial incomes could afford the up-market designs of Vivienne Westwood from shops such as World's End and Nolstagia of Mud where it cost a king's ransom to look impoverished. Urban vagrancy was a property of 'rich kids' and, by 1983, any youth who had a job was relatively rich; yet it symbolized the confusion of the time.

In a way, the studied scruffiness of the urban vagrants captured the ambiguities and inconsistencies. It was a version of the 'love' tattoo across the fingers of the right hand and 'hate' across the left writ large. Like the youth wearing a CND lapel button next to his swastika or the female with a ring through her nose (the kind with which animals are led to the slaughter) and a radical feminist slogan like 'end rape–castrate men' on her T-shirt.

Not only did the previously sharp lines between subcultures become indistinct, but they themselves were racked with internal contradictions. This was a time of social upheaval. The riots had shown, at least to the participants, that the important issues affecting their lives were not about skin colour or the length of hair or even about how much money your parents had; they were about a society which had energized them with the tantalizing promise of consumer items and left them in a wasteland, their vigour emptying. Perhaps the riots produced no tangible pay-off, but they did succeed in uniting youth into a solid phalanx with an enormous potential for making things happen. What happened was that the media devoted itself for over two weeks to the disorders and the government mounted full-scale investigations in most of the urban centres. To a disenchanted youth whose feeling of impotence had been compounded by a sense of uselessness, this in itself was reward enough for the night's work.

1982 was a relatively quiet year with just one major disturbance in Brixton at the very end of the year. The lull was probably the result of a combination of the optimism that things might improve after the government had formally recognized that youth were protesting about their problems and a feeling of catharsis, the 1981 riots being a sort of purgatory experience with the youths ridding themselves of all their frustrations in two frantic weeks. But during that year, youths started to speak the same language and it was a language of violence, not against each other, but against society; specifically against the symbols of their entrapment.

My ambition in this chapter has been to offer a version of the events leading up to the 1981 riots. I haven't charted actual incidents, though there were plenty of small disturbances building towards the copycat outbreaks and these are neatly summarized in an article by Mary Venner (1981). Instead, I've analysed the broad changes affecting youth: the changes were those occurring as the UK moved from being a post-war affluent society to one racked with economic instability, industrial decline and multiplying unemployment. The process whereby youth was commercialized, packaged and made available as a series of commodities has been crucial in psyching up young people to expect a lot more from society than society has to offer them. Resulting from this has been a disjuncture between expectations and the opportunities available to realize them. The response of young people to this has been self-evident. Riots don't close the gap between what you want and what you can get; and, if they do, it's only for a short time, anyway. The structure of opportunities has, if anything, crumbled even more in the time since summer 1981, and this opens up the big question: what happens next?

Nobody insists that youth be anything but patient and passive. They have shown that, when fired, they are neither. In the next chapter, I'll look at the possibilities for the future.

MARK
WHAT IT'S LIKE NOW

. . . it's 1984. Almost 21, the age when you're meant to be grown up. In a way, you are: you've done two stretches in Winson Green and one in DC. You came out nine months ago after doing three months for burglary. It seemed an easy job; Dave organized it; it was a house in Solihull; looked dead safe. You thought you'd got away with it as well, but, two days later, the old bill came round. They've got your card marked.

That's all in the past though: now you're going to go straight. You're back with your girl, now you're living together with your child, so that makes it important that you stay out of trouble. Your girl hasn't got a job, so you exist on 'social'. It's not easy, but there are millions more in the same situation and, at least, it makes it a bit easier to think that there are better-qualified people than you who are worse off. Trouble is that if there are any jobs at all going, they're more likely to get them. You've got nothing going for you: 21, two CSEs, no experience and a bit of criminal form.

You don't fight so much nowadays: it doesn't seem worth it now. You've had that much aggravation from the law over the years that it's a joke. You see plenty of younger kids who're into beating each other up and the pakis still get smacked about something rotten; but you leave it to the kids. It's not worth it. Anyway, these pakis nowadays are not such mugs as they used to be; they're organized in gangs and they are mostly tooled up. What's worse is that the cops are looking out for white kids as the troublemakers. They won't touch the pakis 'cause they scream, 'it's prejudice, you're just picking on us'.

You can't believe this bullshit about blacks and pakis complaining that the police harass them. It's a load of bollocks. It's the white kids they pick on. They leave the blacks and the pakis alone most of the time. When you and your mates were in the riots in 1981, there were pakis going round even then with baseball bats in the back of their wagon. They got pulled and the cops said: 'What are you doing with these?' And they said: 'We been playing baseball.' And that was it. Your mob wouldn't dare go around with tools. In any case, you were too well known; they took one look at your hair and you were as good as nicked. You think it's a waste of time, nowadays.

Mind you, life's a bit dull without the occasional fight. All it consists of is getting up, usually about twelve, having some breakfast, read the papers, listen to the radio and then go round to Dave. Then you might go to see another mate or go into town. It's useless going to the Job Centre. They never have any jobs, so you might as well save your feet. You wonder what must be going through the mind of some of these young kids leaving school today. If only they knew: what an experience they're in for!

You read a lot about the 'problems', 'anxieties', 'pressures' of young kids on the dole, but, after a while it's not so bad; you just get used to the boredom. You've had plenty of time to adjust. In fact, it would come as a shock to your system if you got a job now. You were in the dole office the other day and some guy came up to you and started asking a few questions – said he was writing a book or something. He said: 'Have you ever thought that you might never get a job, ever?' So you said: 'Well, I never think anything else. I don't know what work means, but there again, you never miss what you haven't had, do you?' You talked to him for hours, but he'll still never know what it's actually like to be in your position. He said he'd been on the dole enough times in the past; but, no matter how many interviews he does, he won't know what it's like *now*. Then there were some jobs about, now's different: there's nothing, no jobs, nothing to hope for.

The boredom is easier to live with after a while. But not having any money doesn't get easier, it gets harder. Over the years, you've learned to adjust: you can never afford new clothes, so you buy them off kids who've lifted them from shops in town; there's less risk of being done that way. But getting food and clothes for your woman and kid is just impossible. It means that you can hardly afford to have a drink at night. Good job you don't smoke; Dave does but he scrounges most of his fags. Living without money is a sort of art you've perfected, not easily though. It means keeping your eyes and ears open for bargains, not buying stuff from shops when you can steal it.

Sometimes, it gets you down and you wish you could afford to go out more, dress better, not have to think about everything you buy. It's tempting when you have to listen to other kids, who've done a blag or something and made off with something. You can usually tell 'cause they're in some smart gear and buying plenty of drinks. Some of the kids are real berks too. You wouldn't think they'd have the sense to do a job. It makes you mad sometimes when you see them. You get home and you feel like screaming and shouting and just smashing the place up. It makes you boil with anger and you just want to destroy something. If your woman happens to be in the way, then she usually cops for it; she's been black and blue with bruises sometimes. You know it's wrong but it's just that you're so mad. Not against her, nor the kids down the pub for that matter; you're not sure who or what you're mad against. All you know is that you're angry about yourself and your situation and you have to let that anger go against something or someone. It doesn't do any good, but what does?

Nothing you can do is going to change the situation you're in now. Tomorrow is going to be pretty much like today and today was like yesterday. You've accepted the fact that you're not going to do much different from what you're doing now for the rest of your life. It used to depress you; now you don't care. It would be nice to think something would change. Still: if it happens, it happens; if it doesn't, it doesn't. And it won't.

-WHAT FUTURE?

STREET LOGIC

It's a mistake to think that the more exotic and visible youths, like skins and urban vagrants, are extreme and unrepresentative of youth generally. Our everyday observations might indicate that a lot of young people are ordinary, dull, passive and not interested in trying to detach themselves from the rest of society. And, of course, a lot of youths move quite smoothly from school to college or university and never get entangled in the more disreputable web of subcultures. But these aren't the kids who go rioting in the urban precincts any more than they are the ones who smash up Asians or the ones who used to rip up cinema seats. Two-thirds of the country's young are workingclass, that's about 5.4 million kids, nearly 2 million of whom have no work. They are the ones to whom things like punk and heavy metal supply relevance. By the time they reach the symbolic age of 21, they're already derelicts. If no job has turned up by then, they're as good as finished because matters don't seem to improve and might even get worse. Even those who do work, are forced to do so for pathetically low wages. This is the social profile of the rioter.

Blacks, in particular, are badly affected. In Brixton, the centre of gravity of the 1981 riots, over half the black youths are out of work; and almost two-thirds of black youths are on the dole in Moss Side, Manchester, another setting for riots in 1981. The educational system is losing credibility rapidly, particularly amongst blacks who regularly falter in exams. They recognize that qualifications are not passports to jobs, but merely pieces of paper. Lyndon, a 19-year-old who had held two jobs in a three-year period after leaving school with four 'O' levels, put it like this: 'Worthless; that's what exams are. I did as well as I could at school. I worked hard. But when you get out there and try to get work, it's a waste of time. I got a job in the meat market for a bit, just humping stuff around; then I got a job as a bookie's clerk. Rubbish. I think all the time I spent at school was a waste. I might as well have done nothing for all the good it's done me.' His reflection on school is typical of many black youths – and who can fault their logic?

In this last chapter, I'm going to try to assess what the future holds for youths, black, white and Asian, not by analysing economic trends, but by uncovering their attitudes and feelings towards the kinds of urgently pressing issues that affect and will continue to affect their lives in a massive way. Beginning with education.

Speculating on the causes of what they see to be a mass demoralization of youth, Lowell Field and John Higley put forward a similar idea to the one I proposed in the last chapter. They express it rather differently stating that the social order works 'by providing opportunities for improving one's occupational and more general social status by clearly specifying reasonable "prices" for such status improvements, and by giving considerable assurance that if the prices are paid improved status will be obtained.' (1982, p. 13).

Changes resulting in climbing youth unemployment have precipitated a scramble of about ten school-leavers for every available job and: 'In the now crowded competition for relatively few desirable positions, the individual finds no reasonable assurance that if the price for improved status . . . is paid such improved status will be obtained.' (1982, p. 13).

The 'price' to be paid is the attainment of educational qualifications, from CSEs to university degrees. These have taken on increasing importance since the war, a process called 'credentialism', meaning that access to jobs and promotions has become more related to paper qualifications. Schools relentlessly emphasize this, devoting a whole structure of careers masters, advisers, etc., to assisting the student in getting a job and getting the requisite qualifications for that job: 'If you want to be a draughtsman, you need GCE 'O' levels in at least four subjects, including technical drawing and maths . . .' etc.

In other words, school-kids are asked to pay the price of working assiduously in their academic studies so that they can pass examinations, gain qualifications and thus manoeuvre their way into advantageous positions in the job market. But, as Field and Higley pointed out, youth are finding 'no reasonable assurance' that they will have their educational efforts rewarded with a job and so align their attitudes to school accordingly. Their reasoning is summed up by Darren, at 17 with six CSEs (one grade 1), and out of work:

> They don't teach you anything of any use at school. It's useless. At school, they get you in and ask you what you want to do. So you take your first pick, say plumbing, then carpentry or engineering. So the teachers tell you what you need (qualifications) and you say, 'all right then'. Anyway, when you take this to your careers office, they say: 'What's all this about then? You can't pick and choose . . . I don't care what qualifications you've got.' And you wonder why you bothered in the first place.

The research of Kenneth Roberts showed that this is a fairly common view: 'Some pupils take the view that qualifications are "no use" – that CSEs and even 'O' levels carry no guarantee of employment', yet, he goes on: 'jobs are the carrots with which teachers recruit and motivate pupils on examination courses.' (1982, p. 21). The contradiction is apparent: if jobs are the carrot for educational motivation and the carrot disappears. . . .

Objectively, even the most modest of qualifications give the school-leaver a slight edge in the labour market and any edge is better than none. Yet who can convince a youth of 20 with four years' dole queue experience under his belt that this is so? 'This is one way in which, it has been argued, youth employment undermines education', writes Roberts. And education will continue to be undermined as school-leavers continue to take their place in the dole queues. Teachers simply can't mislead the youths; as Lacell, an 18-year-old black guy put it: 'They still tell you to get qualifications and the rest of it, but kids know already before thay leave school what it's going to be like after.' The idea's expressed nicely by Tucker Jenkins of Phil Edmonds' TV show *Tucker's Luck* (BBC-2): 'You need three 'O' levels to deliver papers, these days.'

Qualifications have never 'guaranteed' jobs, of course, but, equally, they have never been as voided of their supposed purpose as they are in the 1980s. The threat of unemployment registers in the consciousness of many school-children, like Trevor, 18 and out of work for two years: 'It's a joke, the teachers tell you to work hard and do your homework and all that and, all the time, you've sussed that it's for nothing. Our kid is 20 now and he's had one proper job for four months since he left school (he'd also been on two schemes). I could see what was coming, so I never bothered with school. I suppose I gave up trying when I was about 14 and then I just dossed.'

John didn't spot the futility of the exercise so quickly and opted to stay on at school until he was 18, but, at 20, he saw things more clearly:

> A waste of time; that's what it was staying on at school. I haven't had a real job since I left school and I was pretty well qualified compared to my mates (he had five 'O' levels and one 'A' level in geography). I wish now I hadn't stayed on 'cause I would have been picking up my dole money for two years instead of living off my parents.

Depressing as it sounds, there is a certain logic to his argument; and the logic of the streets is contagious. Listen to Mohammed Akram, 19, unemployed for eighteen months: 'Who wants 'em? CSEs and all the rest of the qualifications are no good to you 'cause there's no jobs when you get 'em. If there were jobs, then you might try to get some exams, but you're better off on the dole nowadays.' £42 every two weeks sounds better than nothing if the end-product is the same. Pragmatic considerations sometimes outweigh all others, including those related to exams and qualifications; as Roy, 18, explained: 'I left school before my exams 'cause it meant that, if I stayed on till June, I couldn't draw any money off the dole till September. So I left early and signed straight on.'

As well as undermining education, unemployment tends to break the link between what's learned at school in terms of theoretical and practical skills and what goes on in the 'real' world of work. They begin to seem like two separate and unrelated realms. Steven, 18 and out of work for two years:

> I've learned more in the two years since I left school than I did all the time at school. They don't teach anything that you can use when you leave. I've forgotten most of it, no *all* of it, since I left. It's no use to you at all I don't think. If a kid came up to me and asked me what to do about school, I'd tell him, 'get out', 'cause it's not gonna be any use.

In a similar vein, Dean: 'They teach you nothing at all about the important things in life: about how hard it is to get a job and what work's like and how to go about getting a job and all that. You start learning when you leave school.'

Apart from the obvious gearing-down of aspirations and a general demotivation, an important consequence of these changes in attitudes towards education is truancy. Because of their perfectly legitimate appraisal of the limited use of education, kids simply refuse to waste their time at school: the immediate gratification of every impulse becomes a part of their life-style and they see no point in pursuing long-term objectives which will, in all probability, never materialize. Peter, 17:

> I left school when I was 14 as far as I'm concerned. I never used to tell the old lady, of course, but I used to skive off, just hanging around town for most of the day. I couldn't see the point in what they taught you at school. . . . I knocked around with kids from my school and a few others who were out of work – now I'm one of them, eh?

Like Peter, many youths opt out of school one or two years before the official school-leaving time. Their approach sums up the declining will not only to work at school, but to go to school at all. The loss of motivation is born out of the contradiction of being taught skills that will be irrelevant and of being exhorted to gain qualifications whose market value is diminished by the contracting number of jobs available.

Education has traditionally been linked quite closely to the requirements of the labour market; now the link has been loosened, if not broken. Whether youth will recover the will to be educated and to participate actively in that process is uncertain. What is certain is that, so long as unemployment continues to damage their life chances, they will weigh up the costs and benefits involved and will conclude that the 'prices' to be paid for improvements are not justified by the rewards available after leaving school.

GIVING UP

'Adjustment to unemployment by giving up appears to have been the dominant response in the thirties', according to the psychologist Marie Jahoda (1982, p. 92). After reviewing the research, she concludes that the most common response to the prolonged depression was to become apathetic, discouraged and to cease looking for work.

Nowadays, this may not be an option available to a man or a woman with a young family and plenty of responsibilities; but it is most definitely one being taken up by the young. Some not only give up the search for jobs, but surrender their willingness to enter employment at all; like Chris, aged 20: 'I've got no ambition left, I just read all day. No televison or anything. I've got no plans for work now. I just drift around. There's no point in getting a job anyway. I don't want one.' Nick was less insistent, but remained selective after just eight months out of work. As a punk, he was 'anti-authority' and believed in 'self-expression and anarchy'; so certain jobs didn't suit him: 'I don't particularly want a job. . . . If it was this or having a job in a factory getting bored . . . I'd prefer this.'

Chris's resignation was one extreme type of response to a protracted period of unemployment. He was a 1983 version of the hippies: he'd revised any ideas about working he might have had when leaving school and 'drifted', as he put it, ever since. He felt himself to be an outcast and wanted it that way. Both he and Nick had dropped the objective of getting a good job and abandoned the means of getting it – retreatists in Merton's terms.

Others, such as Stephen, a 20-year-old black guy, would do 'anything' to work. I asked him what he would do if he were offered £5 more than he got off the dole to do a job labouring: 'I'd take it. I would take anything they (the Department of Employment) offered me now 'cause doing something is better than doing nothing.'

'Doing something' was a preferable alternative to the mind-numbing boredom being out of work entailed and he'd been out for a total of four years: 'I used to get depressed about it, but I've come out of that now. Something will break this sooner or later. But it's out of my control though.'

The reasoning behind this is similar to that behind George Orwell's dictum: 'Cease to use your hands and you have lopped off a huge chunk of consciousness.' (1975, p. 173). But it isn't a reasoning shared by many other youths. They may feel degraded, frustrated and impotent because of their inactivity, but, for the most part, they feel work is for earning money. It's purely a matter of economic necessity. Another black youth, Lacell, when asked the same question as Stephen, responded: 'No, I wouldn't do *anything*, and I won't be just cheap labour.'

Nobody wants to submit themselves to the tyranny of working in unpleasant jobs for poor wages and most youths refuse to. But then again, it's an employer's market and, when firms can offer £55 per week for a labourer and still find thirty or forty kids queuing at the personnel office, then they're unlikely to be concerned about things like job enrichment or raising wages. There are plenty of people like Stephen, willing to do the job in preference to 'doing nothing'.

Jahoda's research indicates that there are several modes of adaptation to the kind of long-term unemployment that's now afflicting modern youth; unemployment is too predictable. They'd be more shocked if they got a job straight away – or at all. The other responses are more prevalent. For example, fear and distress, numbness, adaptation to circumstances and weakening hope. Youths, being mostly resourceful people, adapt to their situation and settle into a life of worklessness so that they may eventually come to think like Joe, 18 and two years out: 'I don't know what it's like to work. I can't even think about it. I'm happy the way I am, mind you. It's all right getting up late and dossing about. I don't know if I could stand a job now, I've got so used to this way. I'm all right.'

Yet all the time, hope is weakening and the futility of even thinking about a job strengthens. 'It's hopeless unless you want to be cheap labour for £40 a week and I'm not doing that 'cause, by the time they take your tax out and the rest of your stoppages, you're better off here (on the dole)', reasoned John, a 20-year-old. On the subject of whether he'd given up trying, he said:

Yeah, it took a while and you start off hoping that you're gonna get another job (he did a three-year apprenticeship in electrical engineering), but then you don't see any going and there are no interviews, so you think it's all a complete waste of time and you give up hoping. That's exactly how I feel now: there's no point in trying . . . no matter what you do, factories are still closing every week.

So how about the various work training schemes in operation? These would seem to be an acceptable stop-gap, keeping the youths' hands (and minds) busy, providing them with some purposeful activity and rewarding them financially with slightly more than they would draw in unemployment benefits. (Details on and the criticism of the structure and operation of these schemes can be found in Rees and Atkinson, 1982.) Let me just state that schemes such as the Wider Opportunities Courses (WOC) and, later, the Youth Opportunities Programme (YOP) were initiated and funded by the government with the intention of easing the unemployment situation, to help young people gain jobs where possible and, according to James McGuire and Philip Priestley, 'to equip them for and keep them attuned to the world of work where prospects of employment were actually more distant' (1982, p. 17).

The YOP, which succeeded the Job Creation Projects of the mid-1970s, made funds available to local government bodies and other agencies for the running of job placement schemes and part-time training programmes for out-of-work youths. The Youth Training Scheme (YTS) superseded it in 1983. About a quarter of a million people are estimated to be on YOPs or YTSs or affiliated projects; they constitute the single largest body of individuals ever given any form of 'life skills' training; about 70 per cent of under 18-year-olds are on them in 1984. The concept of 'life skills' is a rather vague one and one which wasn't attended to that carefully by the Manpower Services Commission, the government body responsible for funding and directing the programmes. As a result, the tutors meant to be disseminating knowledge on life skills often tended to fall back onto a sort of remedial education, including liberal general studies.

The schemes, particularly YOP, have been under attack from many quarters, most of the criticism centring around their abuse by firms for exploiting youths. I want to consider the reactions of some youths who have been on the schemes.

Take Peter, 18, whose views were fairly typical: 'Slave labour. That's what they are. You won't catch me on one again. Okay, they don't work you that hard, but you've got to be there and the pay's no good. I wouldn't go on another.' Slave labour is the key term used time and again by youths involved, who feel they are exploited quite openly and, sometimes, ruthlessly, by the programmes. 'I went on one', said William, a 20-year-old rasta, 'I was doing slab-laying. But it was no good. They make you work for nothing. I wouldn't go on another one.'

Some youths simply refused to partake in the schemes because of the same basic reason. Dean, 17: 'I'd do any job, anything. But I wouldn't do a YOP or YTS scheme. The old man wouldn't let me, anyway. We both reckon it's a form of cheap labour.'

Apart from the exploitation sensed by youths on the schemes there is the problem of linking what they learn there to work. In fact, what they learn on the schemes may not be that appreciable, as Stephen remarked: 'All I learned on the job training scheme was how to make a good cup of coffee.' Extreme perhaps, but the sentiment is shared by a great many other youths who feel they gain little in terms of knowledge or experience from YOPs. Andrew: 'I can just about make a screw and a screwdriver. That's all.'

As well as this intrinsic criticism, there is an extrinsic one, summed up by Darren, 17: 'I went on a YOP scheme for technicians not long after I left school. I was working for six months. My parents were quite pleased. The problem is that when that six months was up, I was out of work again.' As with conventional education, the credibility of government training schemes and their ability to command and sustain the motivation of participants is undermined by the apprehension that, when it's all over, there is no job. Back to square one.

Many youths, especially black youths, sense that if they have any future at all, it lies in entrepreneurial activity. Self-employment isn't so much a goal embodied in the Protestant ethic, but a last desperate effort to make ends meet when nothing else is available. In some circumstances, it might be an ideal, something to be placed alongside a career in the professions, a position to command status and the respect of others. Not in this situation. Richard, 20, encapsulated the feeling:

> The situation's gonna get worse. I'm sure of it; there's no hope of it improving. I've been out now for two-and-a-half years, so I think the only way to do something is to start contracting . . . be self-employed. My old man did that; he got made redundant from his factory job, so he employed himself as self-employed and he's doing all right at it. I'll do that I suppose, get myself some jobs slabbing. That's about all there is left.

Well, it's not quite 'all there is left' because some resourceful and not entirely honest youths make alternative arrangements to solve their economic problems. They continue to sign on and declare themselves available for employment, but they illicitly take a job, working without making official declarations for 'money in the hand'. Sometimes, the employment is a sideline and the youth works only part-time or on an occasional basis. Other times, it may be a virtual full-time job, as it was with Willie, who fitted false ceilings six days a week and took an hour off to sign on every two weeks. 'I take home about £150 a week and it's all tax-free. Sometimes I get it up to £200' (and I'm interviewing *him*).

Stories of 'moonlighting', or working an additional evening job have circulated for years, as have those of workers on the 'lump'. Unemployment has led to a further growth in the black economy and young people who are registered as unemployed zealously seek out work so that they can augment their dole Giros. If this continues to grow, it will present a rather serious issue with unemployed young people surrendering themselves to an openly exploitative arrangement in which the employer pays less than adequate day-rates (about £20 per day average) and offers none of the usual protections afforded by National Insurance, superannuation, etc. Apart from this, it is simply illegal, so both the employee and employer are breaking the law by entering into the arrangement.

Not that youths working in this way consider themselves to be lawbreakers; they simply see the black working as an expedient, just a way to make those ends meet. There are, however, more openly illegal ways of accomplishing this and, in the next section, I'm going to look at some of the build-ups to law-breaking.

NOTHING TO LOSE

The 'innovators' in Merton's theory were those who carried on pursuing the goals set for them by society, but devised new, illegitimate methods of getting them. They accepted the ends but not the means. So, a person may value the success he or she is meant to strive for, they may desire the kinds of trappings of the consumer society associated with success, but simply not have the means available for getting them. Deprived of money through lack of work and with no other options open, they innovate by breaking certain rules to reach their goals. Crime is an obvious innovation; if you can't afford that video that the ads are constantly telling you is essential nowadays, then steal it. When all else fails, turning to crime is the organizing principle of a great many youths.

Common sense tells us that there is a relationship between unemployment and the incidence of crime, particularly against property. As people get poorer, they tend to look to ways of ameliorating that condition. But the exact nature and strength of the relationship is not so clear. For example, it could be that the poorer people are, the less power they have; thus they are easy prey for zealous policemen and are less able to insulate themselves from the law more thoroughly.

Let's put it this way: unemployment increases the probability that young people will get their names onto a charge sheet. This isn't dismissing the argument that there is a strong relationship between crime and unemployment: it's simply recognizing that there are other factors at work, such as power, which complicate the issue. Nevertheless, there is evidence to suggest that unemployment leads to increases in criminal activity, such as that of Harvey Brenner, who drew up a strong statistical association between the two based on American data (1976). About the young, L. Phillips and his colleagues concluded that any attack on crime must take careful consideration of the 'employment problems facing young people' (1972). It would seem that unemployment particularly affects youths' propensity to engage in crime. An adult with responsibilities to his family and financial commitments might be less prepared to take the risks connected with crime unless the gamble is worth his while; a youth without such trammels may take risks for rather insignificant pay-offs. As did Joe, who'd 'done a shop' in order to steal cigarettes: 'We did it 'cause we thought we could sell the fags. It was no problem breaking into the place, I never even thought about the risks involved at the time; it was a piece of piss.'

Derek on the other hand, at 21, had accumulated some form between the ages of 14 and 18, but had 'reformed'. He married, had two children and held down a steady job as an engineer for eighteen months. Then, he got made redundant, had a short spell maintaining lifts and got laid off again. Desperate to sustain the standard of living he'd established, he considered more serious crime: 'I'm getting a shooter and gonna do a Post Office. It's got to be the way soon. I've thought about it long and hard and I'm not gonna do any good; there's no work about at all and I'm getting deeper in debt. I can do a job and clear everything.' And if you get caught? 'So what? If I draw two years, I've lost nothing. The wife can look after the kids. Social (security) will give her money – more than I can probably give her. I'm gonna be on the dole doing fuck all for the next two years, anyway, the way I see it.'

The risk factor seems to recede in the minds of those subjected to long periods of inactivity. John was a case in point; asked if he'd commit crime, he answered: 'Why not? Really, you've got nothing to lose. You might as well try a job and get some money. And why not? If you get caught and you get locked up, so what? It's like being in a prison being trapped in the house with nothing to do all day in any case.' His statement has a depressing, but plausible consistency to it.

Crime among the young is intimately related to both the poverty unemployment brings and the accent on consumerism covered in the last chapter. Shoplifting used to be the dominant crime of the young and, as Anne Campbell pointed out: 'The crime statistics for shoplifting reflect the rapid increase in the affluence and materialism of the sixties. . . . In absolute terms, it (shoplifting amongst the young) increased by 274 per cent in those years (1960–66)' (1981, pp. 119–20). On the more recent situation, Campbell wrote: 'Put bluntly, teenagers whose style and self-concept have come to depend on buying power and subcultural knowledge of the right thing to buy will be driven to theft when economic circumstances demand it,' (1981, p. 120).

The previous chapters indicate the extent of youths' dependence on the consumable products of the affluent society. Today's kids have been weaned to want. Deprive them of the ability to translate those 'wants' into 'haves' and they start to formulate alternatives. In the last chapter, I discussed some of the more dramatic consequences, but a resort to crime, perhaps on a steady, routinized basis is a probability. What's more, the reasoning behind the decision to turn to crime and the balancing of alternatives is sometimes difficult to find fault with. Two years inside with your wife provided for by the state, or two years of struggle on the dole? A spell in DC or Borstal doing nothing, or a continuation of an endless sentence of boredom?

Campbell's book, *Girl Delinquents*, highlights the extra pressures on girls in forcing them towards crime. 'As a group, women have historically been preoccupied with appearance – and with good reason', she states, adding that until recent times 'a girl's whole economic future rested on her desirability as a marriage partner for the right male buyer' (1981, p. 120). Females, possibly more than males, are dependent on the market if only because they are brought up with calls to buy cosmetics, clothes and jewellery to enhance their looks ringing in their ears. The effect of this on girls has been analysed by, amongst others, Angela McRobbie and Jenny Garber, who trace the experience of girls in relation to youth subcultures where their role is one of 'structured secondariness' (1975, p. 211). Most youth subcultures, certainly up to the mid-1970s, were male-focused with females occupying only marginal positions. McRobbie, in her analysis of the magazine *Jackie*, illustrates the way in which girls orient their lives around fantasizing over pop stars, listening to records and striving to keep their boyfriends (1982). In one passage, she presents the case of a young female who stole from a shop in order to give her boyfriend an expensive and therefore impressive birthday present.

The point these writers make is that females are even more susceptible to the pressures of the market and the forces of consumerism than their male counterparts and may be more inclined towards crime, especially petty theft, in the type of severe economic circumstances brought about by unemployment. Penny, 17, was a fairly regular 'tea leaf' (thief) since she was 'about 9', successful in the sense that she had never been so much as apprehended by the police: 'I suppose you get cleverer at it the more you do it. I like to have nice clothes and keep looking good. . . . I never had any money, so I started lifting and kept on doing it.' It's as simple as that.

Roz, 19, had 'been away' a couple of times for theft, but saw it very much part of her life: 'Quite honestly, if I didn't do a bit of tea-leaving now and again, I'd never have clothes or make-up or anything – I'd be a wreck.' (Neither girl had ever worked in a full-time job.)

The reasons given by females why they get involved in thieving are not dissimilar to those given by their male counterparts. Often it is a pure matter of expedience: if you want some product and some of your friends already have the product and you haven't the money to pay for it, then you take it. The explanation may sound simplistic and naive, but my purpose isn't to offer a theory of deviance; it's merely to present the perspective of the youths involved. They steal not because of any implicit thrill they get out of the act, but because they live in a culture in which possessions are highly valued and are used as a measurement of personal worth. In an age of consumerism, you are what you have. Their morale already depressed by the lack of meaningful employment, many youths find the absence of clothes, records and the other items of the youth industry intolerable so involve themselves in stealing. The commission of the act of theft is facilitated by the youths' weighing up the possibilities: if he or she gets caught and has to serve a sentence, (if not directly, after non-payment of fines), then it isn't seen as such a bad alternative to life on the dole. In some cases, a spell inside is seen as preferable. This links together with the power of consumerism in the example of Stuart, who at 21 had experienced life in detention centres, Borstals and prisons. Fresh out of Winson Green for 'TDA' (taking and driving away a motor vehicle), he was charged after getting involved in a pub fight: 'They fined me £120 or thirty days. So I took the thirty days. 'cause I wanted to buy this leather flying jacket that cost £150 . . . I was fucking mad 'cause I got that nicked a week after I'd bought it, as well.'

To the rapidly hardening recidivist, thirty days is, as Stuart put it, 'a piece of piss'. When a life out of work is punctuated by periods in institutions, then one alternative sometimes has no clear-cut priority over another. Mike, 21: 'I got done for burglary; drew six months for that; pissed myself laughing.' What he knew and the magistrates didn't was that the unfreedom of prison life was not so different from the unfreedom associated with being out of work and, as he added, 'you get your meals regular and it costs nothing'.

Worklessness feeds crime and, as Iain Crow pointed out: 'The great danger is that amongst the growing number of young unemployed of today we are building up the stage army of recidivists who will fill our prisons in years hence.' (1982, p. 5). Related to this is the additional problem that having a criminal record, particularly a long and serious one including prison sentences, makes it even harder to get a job. And when jobs are scarce, it makes getting work a virtual impossibility. So what do you do? Turning back to crime becomes a probable tactic. And then you get caught and so on and so forth on the downward spiral.

DOLE TECHNICIANS

Depressing conclusions to a book which covers the exuberance and optimism of the 1950s and the apparently boundless affluence of the 1960s. The 1970s were a tightening straightjacket and now the 1980s: what do they promise? Already we have seen rioting in the streets as young people vented their anger. At the other extreme we have a sort of retreatism with youths involving themselves in the dark pleasures of solvent abuse. Glue-sniffing: young people seeking some kind of artificial escape from what was earlier described as 'X-rated reality' by inhaling the toxic fumes of solvents. This is the latest attempt to retreat from an increasingly unpleasant world by inducing altered states of consciousness. Youth has been through a whole cycle of dope from amphetamines to LSD; the rich kids snort coke, the poor dip their noses into plastic bags filled with glue. How fitting that workingclass youth are seeking their escape via the legitimate commercial products of glue manufacturers. It's as if they're saying: 'Go on then, try it! Ban Bostik. Illegalize one of the products *everybody* uses.'

Both rioting and sniffing glue are the attempts of young people who feel unfit or rejected to solve their problems. The problems used to be the ones inherited from the workingclass generally: routine, low-paid, meaningless jobs, a bleak uninspiring leisure life and limited prospects.

Now there are more specific, newly-created problems manufactured not just out of their class position, but out of their lack of work and their youth. Young people are amongst the hardest hit by rising unemployment. They will continue to leave school and be immediately conscripted to the army of dole queuers. They will have no comprehension of what it's like to get up in the morning, do a day's work and be rewarded, however inadequately on Thursday night.

The sense of fatalism is spreading like a plague amongst modern youth; they feel – quite rightly – that they simply have no say in their futures, a view captured nicely by Geoff, 17:

Whatever you do and no matter how hard you try to get a job, you ain't gonna get one. I went for three interviews in the first month I signed on; since then, not one (he'd been out of work eighteen months). You can't kid me there's any work about. Who's gonna want me, anyway? No qualifications and no experience. I might as well forget it. It ain't getting any better but there's fuck all *I* can do about it.

The temporary relief afforded by such measures as sniffing glue or stealing or even rioting are exactly that: temporary. They are in no sense effective in nullifying the devitalizing fatalism that's draining youth of their sense of purpose and control. Rioting for one or two nights breaks the monotony and at least restores some semblance of efficacy: it makes young people feel that they can actually produce changes, even if small and insignificant ones. But riots have only limited utility in bringing short relief from inactivity, boredom and the loss of self-control. So too do such things as getting doped up and slipping into a different consciousness, or supplementing your income with the fruits of theft or illicit work. Yet, in a way, all these things have a purpose in that they force some public recognition of the circumstances under which young people live; they bring at least a perspective on the problems faced by young people.

A six-month study in Birmingham in 1981 found that unemployed school-leavers went through periods of despair and pessimism into a phase of resignation and apathy (Stokes, 1981). Young people had no inclination to look for a job after repeated failures and so gave up. Nowadays, they don't even have a sequence of failures because they don't get sent to job interviews. But, the mood of resignation brought out by the study is still there and growing.

The study was conducted before the riots and concluded that an increase in criminal behaviour as the pay-off of the mood of resignation was inevitable. While this may be so, we can't dismiss the possibility that there will be repeats of the 1981 urban riots. The Birmingham study interpreted a diffused hostility against the community in the absence of any tangible target to blame for the youths' situation. This hostility is presumably what was converted into violent action. So will it convert again?

There is unquestionably a large amount of hostility submerged beneath the ostensibly dull and passive surface appearance of many youths. Those worst affected by the economic squeeze are predictably the more hostile – not always, but mainly. It could remain submerged; then again it could manifest itself in violence, either of a mass variety or violence focused on specific groups.

In chapter 4, I wrote of the skinhead mentality, that outlook shared by many youths in which Asians and, to a much lesser extent blacks, are selected as targets for attack. Their selection is based on the process of scapegoating and they are blamed for all manner of social evil; unemployment is a major one. The attribution of blame to Asians, visibly different 'outsiders', is nothing new, but has a persistent quality and it looks like persisting through the 1980s. In the 1950s and the 1960s, territory was used as the basis for rivalry, with gangs from different localities fighting each other. This has been replaced or, at least, augmented by racism. Asians, in the skinheads' mentality, simply can't be part of their territory; even if they live next door, they're still outsiders.

On the surface, the skins might have disappeared, but the racist mentality which provided the motor of the subcultures most certainly hasn't. What's more, many youths feel quite self-righteous about their outlook and sense that the majority of the rest of society are solidly behind them – 'I got copped for shooting a paki with my air rifle, but the copper let me off 'cause it was only a paki' – and they may be right.

The racist hostility will continue and Asians will remain the butts. Asians have retaliated (as Mark's story reminds us) and will marshall themselves in the interests of self-protection. A type of inter-ethnic rivalry between white youths attempting vainly to resurrect workingclass traditions and Asians seeking self-preservation looks set to continue. The organization called the Anti-Paki League (APL) may not survive, but the sort of mentality that gives rise to such movements remains as vital and vigorous as ever.

Yet the 1981 riots showed that the rage built up by continual frustration is not necessarily directed towards scapegoated groups; there can be a sudden discharge of energies against the whole system generating the problems of youth. Like most other attempts to challenge the social order, the riots were largely of symbolic value. They were least effective in prompting actual material improvements, most effective in demonstrating that young people were not passive absorbers of pressures, but active reactors to them. The property the youths vandalized, the shops they looted, the authorities they attacked were all symbolic targets; they symbolized the system that worked against their best interests.

Once that perception had been reached, that is that the problem of unemployment and relative poverty were *not* caused by specific groups, then angry and frustrated youths forgot their differences and united to attack any tangible manifestation of that system. Disregard the argument that these were 'race riots': they were youth riots. The criterion of unity was youth; people felt they shared common problems, were involved in common issues and could at least share an effort at confronting them, albeit a vain effort.

But even if the unity hewn out of the perception of common problems is not lost on many urban youth, the overriding concern under deteriorating conditions is with 'number one': yourself. Rick was 18, out of work 'more or less for two years'; he saw clearly the problems besetting youth: 'There's no point in blaming pakis, blacks or anybody else; the government is to blame for all this. But, what do you do? You've got no time to worry about anybody most of the time. You're too busy looking after number one.'

As we approach the midpoint of the 1980s, many voice profound concern about the future of youth. At the extreme there is the feeling that the entire social and moral fabric could be ripped to shreds by a whole generation of unruly youths This is, of course, an exaggeration. Gearing up social control operations, particularly in 'trouble' areas like Brixton, and instigating more 'short, sharp shock' treatments are based on the view that youth is threatening. It's not. There will almost certainly be more intermittent disturbances, perhaps on the scale of 1981, if only because there are no signs that there will be improvements in the position of young people. Yet, after more surges of violent activity in which youths will once more demonstrate their hate and anger, there will be a period of containment.

I mean by this that youths' opposition will be contained by the introduction of more and more training schemes, even rehabilitation programmes, designed to reduce the 'enforced idleness', as Scarman put it, and restore some sense of purpose to young people. These won't resolve any problems, but they will somehow reshape them into a more acceptable form. Subsidies for very low-earners will probably stave off the poverty resulting from continual unemployment, though youths will probably still feature in the two fastest growing crimes, burglary and street offences, both of which are motivated by the desire to get money quickly.

Truancy rates will rise as the credibility of education declines. For the reasons I set out earlier in this chapter, education is set for trouble as more and more school-children begin to put the pieces of the jigsaw together and realize that the jobs that they're supposed to be aiming for, just aren't there. The supposed congruence between the jobs they aspire to and gain qualifications for and the actual jobs available, is illusory. More are understanding this and are reacting quite rationally: 'Why work at school? What for? What's in it for us?' The irony is the educational qualifications are probably more important than ever in giving the youth an edge, however slight, in a congested and competitive labour market.

The scenario sounds depressing. Youths, disenchanted with education, leaving school poorly qualified and moving on to government-funded training courses whilst waiting in vain for 'real jobs' to crop up. Signs are that they won't. So the credibility problem afflicting education will spread upwards to the training programmes.

Beyond all this though, young people are resilient, they're survivors. They will realize that the jobs aren't magically going to reappear, so they'll learn to adapt. Living without work and without purpose is something most of us over 25 find abhorrent. For those younger, it's simply a 'way of life'. They'll be able to live without work; they'll have to. For them the work ethic that's pervaded the western world since the advent of industrial capitalism will be meaningless. Quite soon, many people will reach their mid-twenties with little more than six months' work experience. They won't be interested in rioting any more; they'll have learned to survive by the time they arrive at that stage. Perhaps then the important question will be not 'what's happening to our kids?' (they'll be absorbed into a massive training scheme system), but 'what's happening to our adults?' They're unqualified and inexperienced; the only thing they're good at is surviving.

If there's any benefit to be drawn at all from the horrendous situation confronting youth, it is that we are breeding a new type of resourceful, maybe even inventive, creative being, adept at existing on minimum earnings and able to complement his or her income with bits and pieces from other sources. The youths will learn to extract meaning from the most mundane activities and become skilled at assimilating boredom. Lacking the purpose and, perhaps, direction associated with work, they will acquire the ability to drift through days, weeks, years without targets or goals; just drifting and enduring.

Those of us who have been brought up to believe that the skills and knowledge we acquire are to be applied and practised in some useful context will have to think again when we consider the consequences of the present situation for youth. There seems to be little utility in many of the training programmes and schemes. Increasingly, the only occupational roles available to the young is what one youth, in describing both himself and his generation, called *dole technicians*.

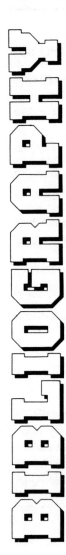

ASHTON, John (1983), 'The children of the welfare state', *New Society*, vol. 64, no. 1066 (21 April), pp. 109–10.

BARNES, Richard (1979), *Mods*, London: Eel Pie.

BARSTOW, Stan (1982), *A Kind of Loving*, London: Corgi.

BOGDANOR, V. and SKIDELSKY, R. (eds.) (1970), *The Age of Affluence*, London: Macmillan.

BRAKE, Mike (1980), *The Sociology of Youth Culture and Youth Subcultures*, London: Routledge & Kegan Paul.

BRENNER, M.H. (1976), *Estimating the Costs of National Economic Policy*, Joint Economic Committee of Congress, Washington DC: US Government Printing Office.

BROOM, Leonard, SELZNICK, Philip and DARROCH, Dorothy (1981), *Sociology*, 7th edn., New York: Harper & Row.

CAMPBELL, Anne (1981), *Girl Delinquents*, Oxford: Basil Blackwell.

CARTER, Angela (1983), 'The recession style', *New Society* (13 January).

CASHMORE, E. (1981), 'After the rastas', *New Community*, vol. 10, no. 2 (winter).

CASHMORE, E. (1982), *Black Sportsmen*, London: Routledge & Kegan Paul.

CASHMORE, E. (1983), *Rastaman*, 2nd edn., London: Unwin Paperbacks.

CASHMORE, E. and TROYNA, B. (eds.) (1982), *Black Youth in Crisis*, London: George Allen & Unwin.

CLARKE, John (1975), 'The skinheads and the magical recovery of working class community', *Cultural Studies*, vols. 7 and 8, pp. 99–102; also in S. Hall and T. Jefferson (eds.), *Resistance Through Rituals*, London: Hutchinson.

CLARKE, J., HALL, S., JEFFERSON, T. and ROBERTS, B. (1976), 'Subcultures, cultures and class', in S. Hall and T. Jefferson (eds.), *Resistance Through Rituals*, London: Hutchinson.

CLOWARD, R.A. and OHLIN, L.E. (1960), *Delinquency and Opportunity*, Glenco, Ill.: Free Press.

COHEN, Albert K. (1955), *Delinquent Boys*, Glencoe, Ill.: Free Press.

COHEN, Philip (1972), 'Subcultural conflict and working class community', *Working Papers in Cultural Studies*, no. 2 (spring), Birmingham: University of Birmingham.

COHEN, Stanley (1980), *Folk Devils and Moral Panics*, 2nd edn., Oxford: Martin Robinson.

CORRIGAN, Paul (1979), *Schooling the Smash Street Kids*, London: Macmillan.

CROW, Iain (1982), 'The unemployment/crime link', *Unemployment Unit Bulletin*, no. 4 (July).

DOWNES, David (1966), *The Delinquent Solution*, London: Routledge & Kegan Paul.

DWORETZKY, John P. (1982), *Psychology*, St Paul, Minn.: West Publishing.

FIELD, G. Lowell and HIGLEY, John (1982), 'The population surplus', *Times Higher Educational Supplement*, (15 January).

FIELD, Simon (1982), 'Urban disorders in Britain and America', in S. Field and P. Southgate, *Public Disorder*, London: Home Office Research Study, no. 72.

FRITH, Simon (1978), *The Sociology of Rock*, London: Constable.

FRITH, Simon (1981), 'Dancing in the streets' *Time Out*, no. 570 (20–26 March).

GILROY, Paul (1982), 'Police and thieves', in CCCS, *The Empire Strikes Back*, London: Hutchinson.

GRIFFITHS, Trevor (1982), *Oi! For England*, London: Faber & Faber.

HALFIN, Ross and MARKOWSKI, Pete (1982), *The Power Age*, London: Eel Pie.

HALL, Stuart and JEFFERSON, Tony (1976), *Resistance Through Rituals*, London: Hutchinson.

HARROP, M., ENGLAND, J.and HUSBANDS, C. (1980), 'The bases of National Front support', *Political Studies*, vol. 27, no. 2.

HEBDIGE, Dick (1979), *Subculture: the meaning of style*, London: Methuen.

HEBDIGE, Dick (1981), 'Skinheads and the search for white working-class identity', *New Socialist*, September/October.

IRR (1981), *Police Against Black People*, London: Institute of Race Relations.

JAHODA, Marie (1982), *Employment and Unemployment: a social-psychological analysis*, Cambridge: Cambridge University Press.

KENNISTON, Kenneth (1968), *Young Radicals*, New York: Harcourt, Brace and World.

KENNISTON, Kenneth (1975), 'Prologue: youth as a stage of life', in R. Havighurst and P. Dreyer (eds.), *Youth*, Chicago: University of Chicago Press.

LARKIN, Ralph W. (1979), *Suburban Youth in Cultural Crisis*, New York: Oxford University Press.

LEBZELTER, G. (1980), 'Henry Hamilton Beamish and the Britons', in K. Lunn and R. Thurlow (eds.), *British Fascism*, London: Croom Helm.

LEE, G. and WRENCH, J. (1981), *In Search of a Skill*, London: Commission for Racial Equality.

McGUIRE, James and PRIESTLEY, Philip (1982), *Life After School*, Oxford: Pergamon Press.

McROBBIE, Angela (1982), 'Jackie: an ideology of adolescent femininity', in B. Waites, T. Bennett, and G. Martin (eds.), *Popular Culture: past and present*, London: Croom Helm.

McROBBIE, Angela and GARBER, J. (1975), 'Girls and subcultures', in S. Hall and T. Jefferson (ed.), *Resistance Through Rituals*, London: Hutchinson.

MARSH, Peter (1977), 'Dole-queue rock', *New Society*, vol. 39, no. 746 (20 January), pp. 112–14.

MARSH, Peter (1978), *Aggro*, London: Dent.

MARSH, P., ROSSER, E. and HARRE, R. (1978), *The Rules of Disorder*, London: Routledge & Kegan Paul.

MARWICK, Arthur (1982), *British Society Since 1945*, Harmondsworth: Penguin.

MELLY, George (1970), *Revolt into Style: the pop arts in Britain*, London: Allen Lane.

MERTON, Robert K. (1969), 'Social structure and anomie', in D. R. Cressey and D.A. Ward (eds.), *Delinquency Crime and Social Process*, New York: Harper & Row.

MUNGHAM, Geoff and PEARSON, Geoff (eds.) (1976), *Working Class Youth Culture*, London: Routledge & Kegan Paul.

MURDOCK, Graham and TROYNA, Barry (1981), 'Recruiting racists', *Youth in Society*, no. 60 (November).

ORWELL, George (1975), *The Road to Wigan Pier*, Harmondsworth: Penguin.

PHILLIPS, L., VOTEY, H. and MAXWELL, W. (1972), 'Crime, youth and the labour market', *Journal of Political Economy*, vol. 80.

RAMPTON, A. (1981), *Committee of Inquiry into the Education of Children of Minority Groups, West Indian Children in our Schools: interim report*, London: HMSO.

REES, T. and ATKINSON, P. (1982), *Youth, Unemployment and State Intervention*, London: Routledge & Kegan Paul.

ROBERTS, Kenneth (1982), 'Contemporary youth unemployment', *British Association for the Advancement of Science*, annual meeting, Liverpool: University of Liverpool.

ROGERS, Dave (1982), *Rock 'n' Roll*, London: Routledge & Kegan Paul.

RUNNYMEDE TRUST AND THE RADICAL RACE STATISTICS GROUP (1980), *Britain's Black Population*, London: Heinemann Educational Books.

SCARMAN, The Rt. Hon. The Lord (1981), *The Brixton Disorders, 10–12 April 1981*, London: HMSO.

SEABROOK, Jeremy (1982), *Unemployment*, London: Quartet Books.

SEABROOK, Jeremy (1983), 'The crime of poverty', *New Society*, vol. 64, no. 1065 (14 April) pp. 63–4.

SOUTHGATE, Peter (1982), 'The disturbances of July 1981 in Handsworth, Birmingham', in S. Field and P. Southgate, *Public Disorders*, London: Home Office Research Study, no. 72.

STEINBERG, Ira (1982), *The New Lost Generation*, Oxford: Martin Robertson.

STOKES, G. (1981), *Unemployment Among School-Leavers*, Birmingham: University of Birmingham.

TAYLOR, M. (1981), *Caught Between: a review of researching into the education of pupils of West Indian origin*, Berkshire: NFER–Nelson.

TAYLOR, S. (1981), 'The far right fragment', *New Society* (28 March).

THOMAS, Michael (1973), 'The wild side of paradise', *Rolling Stone* (19 June).

TOMLINSON, Sally (1980), 'The educational performance of ethnic minority children', *New Community*, vol. 8, no. 3 (winter), pp. 213–34.

TROYNA, Barry (1982), 'Race and streaming: a case study', *Educational Review*, vol. 30, no. 1.

TUMBER, Howard (1982), *Television and the Riots*, London: British Film Institute.

VENNER, Mary (1981), 'From Deptford to Notting Hill: summer 1981', *New Community*, vol. 9, no. 2 (autumn).

WAITES, B., BENNETT, T. and MARTIN, G. (1982), *Popular Culture: past and present*, London: Croom Helm.

WILLIS, Paul (1977), *Learning to Labour*, Farnborough: Gower.

WHITE, Timothy (1983), *Catch a Fire*, London: Elm Tree.

RECORDS
Anarchy in the UK, 36
Babylon's Burnin', 48
Ghost Town, 53
God Save the Queen, 36
I'm the Man, 78
Long Shot kick the bucket, 33
Luxury Gap, The, 80
Message for Rudie, 54
My Generation, 30
One in Ten, 55
Positive Vibration, 52
Pretty Vacant, 36
Quadrophenia, 53–4
Return of Django, The, 33
Rudie's in Love, 54

MOVIES
Blackboard Jungle, The, 25
Great Rock 'n' Roll Swindle, The, 48
Jubilee, 48
Pressure, 43
Quadrophenia, 53
Rock Around the Clock, 25
Saturday Night and Sunday Morning, 31
UndeRage, 67
Woodstock, 34

BOOKS
Age of Affluence, The, 22
Aggro, 64
Folk Devils and Moral Panics, 54
Girl Delinquents, 99
Rastaman, 50
Rock 'n' Roll, 25
Rules of Disorder, The, 65

PAPERS, MAGS, ETC.
Daily Sketch, 26
Bulldog, 66
Contemporary Affairs Bulletin, 69
Guardian, The, 78
How to Combat a Red Teacher, 66
How to Spot a Red Teacher, 66
Jackie, 99
New Community, 49
Nationalism Today, 68
Spearhead, 67

TV SHOW
Tucker's Luck, 91

PLAY
Oi! For England, 67